POLICY ESSAY NO. 4

ENCOURAGING
DEMOCRACY

WHAT ROLE FOR
CONDITIONED AID?

WITHDRAWN

Joan M. Nelson
with Stephanie J. Eglinton

Overseas Development Council
Washington, DC

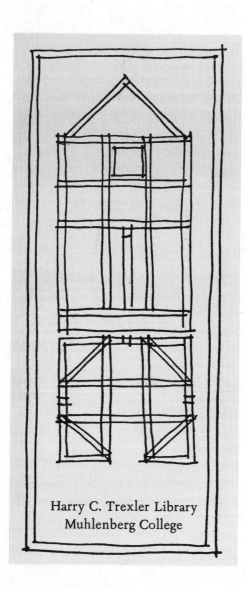

Harry C. Trexler Library
Muhlenberg College

. . . .

ENCOURAGING
DEMOCRACY:

WHAT ROLE FOR
CONDITIONED AID?

Library of Congress Cataloging-in-Publication Data

Nelson, Joan M.
          Encouraging democracy: what role for conditioned aid?/Joan M. Nelson with Stephanie J. Eglinton.

Policy Essay: No. 4
          1. Economic assistance—Political aspects. 2. Democracy—Developing countries. 3. Human rights—Developing countries. 4. Developing countries—Politics and government. I. Eglinton, Stephanie J. II. Title. III. Series.

HC60.N444 1992   338.9′1′091724—dc20   92-14033 CIP
ISBN: 1-56517-004-0
Printed in the United States of America.

Director of Publications: Christine E. Contee
Publications Editor: Jacqueline Edlund-Braun
Edited by Melissa Vaughn
Cover and book design by Tim Kenney Design, Inc.

Contents

Foreword . . . . *vi*

Executive Summary **1**

Introduction **6**

    The New International Setting **6**

    Approaches to Realizing the New International Objectives . **8**

    Varieties of Conditionality **9**

The New Emphasis on Political Reforms **10**

    The Evolving Consensus on the Need for Political Reforms . **11**

    New Donor Policies **15**

    Are the New Policies Credible? **18**

Lessons from Experience **25**

    U.S. Human Rights Experience **26**

    IMF and World Bank Experience with Economic
    Conditionality **33**

Conditional Aid as a Means for Advancing Different
Political Reforms **39**

    Conditionality and Better Economic Governance **41**

    Conditionality and Human Rights **41**

    Conditionality for Broadened Participation and
    Competitive Democracy **42**

Conditionality as a Tool in Varying Country Circumstances 47

     Aid Independence 47

     Ability to Respond to External Influence 48

     Commitment to Reform 48

     Regional Contrasts 52

Beyond the Conditionality Mode 54

Conclusions 59

Notes 65

Acknowledgements 69

About the Authors 70

About the Overseas Development Council 71

Board of Directors 72

Foreword

The collapse of communism and the end of the Cold War has led policymakers in both rich and poor countries to return to several long-standing issues of intrinsic importance: progress toward democracy, reducing military expenditures, protecting the environment, and focusing development strategies on poor people. Addressing these issues will not be easy and will require substantial policy change by all governments. The debate over how governments and international organizations can best promote reforms in other countries is growing in intensity. Specifically, there are increasing calls to put conditions on financial flows from and to poor countries to promote noneconomic policy reforms in the developing world.

The concept of conditionality is controversial in that it implies the use of leverage or coercion on the part of wealthier nations—usually Northern and Western—to encourage shifts in policy and action within target countries—usually Southern and Eastern. Therefore, along with the scope and limits of conditionality, there is a need to assess the potential for alternative, more consensual approaches to the goals of the new international agenda.

Encouraging Democracy: What Role for Conditioned Aid? considers the potential for using conditionality to encourage and support political reform in recipient countries. Joan Nelson, one of this country's foremost scholars on the *politics* of development, examines the logic of political conditionality, its historical record, and its potential risks and benefits. This essay is the first in a series of systematic examinations of the scope and limits of conditionality that will be issued this year by the Overseas Development Council. Forthcoming *Policy Essays* will focus on the goals of reducing military expenditures, encouraging environmental sustainability, and promoting pro-poor development strategies. All of the essays start from the assumption that conditionality is only one of a broad range of alternative or complementary approaches to these goals.

The *Policy Essay* series provides a forum to authors to express opinions, make predictions, and assess policy ramifications in the field of U.S.-developing country relations. The relatively abbreviated format is short enough to serve as a digestible brief for policymaking yet lengthy enough to allow room for more extended analysis.

The Overseas Development Council gratefully acknowledges The Pew Charitable Trusts for their support of the Democratization and Market-Oriented Economic Reforms project and the Ford Foundation and The Rockefeller Foundation for their support of Council's overall program.

John W. Sewell
President
April 1992

Executive Summary

Throughout history, oppressive government has been one major cause of human suffering. In the post-Cold War era, trends within the poorer nations converge with altered priorities in the industrial democracies to place much greater emphasis on political reforms. These reforms include enhanced respect for human rights, improved governance, and competitive democracy. This essay examines the potential uses and risks of conditions linked to aid as one way in which wealthier nations and international agencies may encourage and support political reform in recipient governments.

A recent wave of policy announcements by industrialized democracies around the globe signals an evolving donor consensus that more attention should be placed on political reforms. Many donors have stated that future allocations of aid will favor political reformers and penalize nonreformers. However, the new policies are likely to lead to ad hoc rather than systematic reallocation of aid for several reasons: 1) total concessional aid levels are declining for many donors; 2) reallocation will be constrained by donors' conflicting foreign policy objectives; 3) donors are divided regarding the priority to accord the new objectives; and 4) political reforms are complex, as countries may make progress in some aspects and lose ground on others. In practice, allocative conditionality is likely to translate into specific conditionality.

Lessons from the past indicate that specific conditions attached to aid can effectively promote certain types of reforms, but they can also incur costs for both recipients and donors. The U.S. effort since the mid-1970s to link aid to respect for human rights offers the most significant experience with political conditionality. Despite general legislation mandating that economic and security assistance be withheld from gross violators of human rights, the U.S. record of conditioning aid on human rights grounds has been inconsistent at best. The difficulties derive from the struggles between the Congress and the executive branch, as well as the fact that human rights objectives are often subordinated to other foreign policy concerns. Over the long run, however, conditionality is one of many influences that has contributed to significant progress in areas such as improved human rights monitoring.

The experience of the World Bank and the International Monetary Fund in requiring specific economic policy reforms also offers valuable lessons for political reforms. In general, their conditions are much more extensive and consistently applied. According to their own assessments, compliance varies substantially depending on the type of policy reform. Compliance rates, for example, are high for measures that can be implemented by a small number of central government officials and low for reforms requiring extensive institutional change. The effectiveness of conditionality also varies with the individual circumstances of the recipient country. Clearly, conditionality is more effective if governments are highly dependent on aid.

Various political goals support each other in many ways, but they may not always go together. For example, under the strains of drug traffickers or ethnic separatists, even firmly democratic governments may compromise human rights. In addition, different forms of conditionality should be applied to different categories of political reform. With respect to human rights, international efforts to deny assistance to governments that regularly violate human rights might substantially reduce the level of abuse over time. Conditionality for improved economic governance is really an extension of economic policy conditionality and is likely to take the same specific forms.

Conditional aid should be used with more restraint in promoting broadened participation and competitive democracy. These goals differ from improved human rights and governance in that they are much broader and complex and will be shaped by civil society, not just by recipient governments. However, conditionality might usefully support political liberalization in certain circumstances breaking a specific policy bottleneck, penalizing blatant anti-democratic moves such as military coups or aborted elections and encouraging democratic breakthroughs by offering a temporary "democratic bonus."

Efforts to influence policy reform must always be tailored to individual country circumstances. Nonetheless, when evaluating the potential for conditional aid, some general observations may be taken into account, such as the degree of aid dependence and the capacity of the recipient government to respond to external pressures. The degree of commitment to reform within in the recipient government is also a factor. Real influence, in the sense of changing governments' behavior and attitudes, is likely to be greatest when reform-minded elements in the recipient government are neither very weak nor very strong. If a government is not committed to reforms, the conditions may be met only superficially and not result in sustained reforms. If the government is already strongly committed to reform, conditions may be superfluous: compliance is high but real influence is small.

Countries that have semi-authoritarian governments but are moving towards increased participation may offer the most significant opportunities for specific political conditions. There is, however, no simple formula for effective conditionality in this diverse group. Countries where authoritarian governments have recently been replaced by elected governments present different problems. In most of these fragile reformers, the elites in power are committed to democratic consolidation, and donors should rely primarily on dialogue and support. There is a special risk in newly democratic countries that reforms insisted on by outsiders may be discredited solely because the external intervention violates newly installed democratic processes. Nevertheless, there may be some opportunities for specific bottleneck-breaking conditionality or temporary incentives. In the case of countries with established democratic systems, political conditionality is inappropriate, despite the strains they may face, because it would interfere with their own democratic processes.

The approaches most likely to promote political reform vary widely by geographic region. In Latin America, with several established democracies and many fragile new democracies, the role of conditionality is quite limited, but persuasion and support can be significant. Asia offers a more mixed profile, including several authoritarian countries where donors' other interests are likely to clash with sustained political conditionality. Political conditionality may be easiest for donors in Africa but should be used with special care.

Conditionality is regarded by recipient countries as an invasion of sovereignty and a reflection of power inequalities. To counter resentments as policies of conditionality increase in the 1990s, donors and recipients need to consider the possibilities for moving beyond traditional modes of conditionality. Truly multilateral approaches in which recipients jointly determine criteria for aid may generate more genuine commitment in recipient countries and less abrasive relations between donor and recipient nations.

Two multilateral arrangements concerning Central America currently provide the clearest example of a move in this direction. The San José Accords and the newly created Partnership for Democracy and Development in Central America include multilateral donor and recipient collaboration and involve some explicit focus on political reforms. The Lomé Convention and the Global Coalition for Africa are other arenas intended to promote more open and egalitarian dialogue between wealthy and poorer nations.

Increased multilateral discussion of political reforms may also increase pressure on the donor nations for consistency in their own actions. Poorer nations note that some policies and practices of the industrialized nations contradict each other and actually discourage reforms in poorer countries.

The essay concludes with recommendations on how conditionality might appropriately and effectively encourage political reforms. Conditions attached to aid are more likely to be effective if they focus on improved economic governance and human rights. In general, dialogue and support are more appropriate means to encourage competitive democracy. Conditionality will also be more effective if donors design specific conditions with the lessons of experience in mind and reserve conditionality for appropriate country circumstances. Donors must also coordinate their actions, most importantly with respect to penalties for human rights abuses, military coups, and aborted elections. In sum, conditionality is a useful complement to other approaches encouraging political reforms—not a strategy in its own right.

Encouraging Democracy: What Role for Conditioned Aid?

INTRODUCTION

■ THE INTERNATIONAL AGENDA for both rich and poor nations has changed rapidly since 1989. Even before the unraveling of communism in Eastern Europe and the Soviet Union, several issues were commanding new or heightened attention: among these were environmental protection, respect for human rights, improved governance, progress toward democracy, and pro-poor development strategies. The collapse of communism and the end of the Cold War dramatically accelerated these trends and added reduced arms expenditures to the new agenda.

Progress toward these goals requires changing the policies and behavior of all national governments. The new international agenda has prompted intense debate on how individual nations and international agencies acting singly or in concert, can best promote reforms in other countries. One key theme in this debate is conditionality—that is, the extent and ways in which aid donors can appropriately and effectively link aid to specific noneconomic policy reforms. This essay explores the scope and limits of conditioned aid as a means to encourage political reforms.

THE NEW INTERNATIONAL SETTING

By the end of the 1980s, several separate and powerful trends and events converged to generate the new international agenda. The most obvious and dramatic set of events was of course the demise of communism in Eastern Europe and the Soviet Union. As Cold War goals and constraints faded, the industrial democracies could give higher priority to other foreign policy objectives.

The new global agenda also reflected the effects of much longer and more diffuse yet equally powerful trends. By the mid-1970s the threats to all nations posed by environmental deterioration and arms proliferation were becoming widely recognized. Growing economic interdependence, rising educational levels, the "information revolution," and the ever-increasing mobility of peoples within and between nations altered public expectations and demands on governments within the poorer nations. The most remote villages now have access to ideas and practices originating elsewhere in the world. Local groups increasingly press for greater freedom and participation, environmental protection, and better governance. These trends were capped by the wave of democratic transitions, first throughout Latin America and more recently in Africa and some Asian nations as well as in Eastern Europe.

Within the industrial democracies, shifts in public opinion and the growing strength of specialized nongovernmental organizations (NGOs) also contributed to the emergence of new priorities. Environmental groups and NGOs concerned to reduce poverty in the developing nations increasingly demand that industrial-country governments use all available instruments, including conditions attached to trade and aid, to protect the environment and provide more opportunity for the poor. Amnesty International and similar groups dedicated to promoting human rights have greatly heightened public awareness of repression. And public opinion insists with growing emphasis that foreign aid, if it is to be provided at all, should not go to corrupt or repressive governments.

Interest in conditionality as an instrument to promote the new agenda reflects still another trend: the extensive use by international and bilateral donors during the 1980s of conditioned aid to promote economic reforms. The real effect of these conditions on the recipients' economic policies is hard to gauge. But many observers perceived them as extremely powerful. Why not, they asked, extend such instruments to other goals, including democratic reforms?

Taken together, these trends add up to a considerable erosion of the concept of sovereignty as a constraint on external intervention in nations' domestic policies. The claims of international norms are expanding, although the precise boundaries where legitimate international concerns must cede to national sovereignty are very much in flux. Industrialized nations as well as poorer ones are increasingly being urged to alter domestic policies to reduce global environmental threats and encourage disarmament. Clearly, however, unequal wealth and power gives some nations a wider array of potential instruments for seeking to influence others.

Encouraging democracy and human rights, protecting the environment, reducing arms expenditures, and encouraging pro-poor development strategies all entail considerable changes in the policies and actions of national governments. International agencies, nongovernmental organizations, and national governments can seek to influence other governments' policies and actions in three main ways: persuasion, support, and pressure.

Persuasion or policy dialogue consists of an effort to convince the target government (or antireform elements within it) that altered policies are in its own best long-term interests. Channels and occasions for persuasion range from formal international conferences through meetings between foreign technical experts and ministry officials to private conversations between foreign ambassadors and political leaders. Persuasion can also be approached through research and analysis, to assess past experience or spell out the implications of alternative courses of action.

The most obvious and direct forms of *support for altered policies* are usually training, technical assistance, and financial aid to help to cover the costs of reforms, such as strengthening an election commission or demobilizing troops. Diplomatic support or concessions may also be helpful in some circumstances. Support can also take less direct but equally important forms, by sustaining or improving economic and social conditions that, in turn, encourage political and environmental reforms.

Pressure also takes varied forms and is exercised through multiple channels. Private voluntary organizations like Amnesty International can exert pressure on a government by releasing accurate information on its actions. Other governments can make it clear that diplomatic relations, trade privileges, aid levels, or debt relief will be affected by the target government's reform efforts. Their leverage obviously varies with their importance to the target government: trade- and aid-dependent nations are much more vulnerable to such pressure. In extreme cases, trade sanctions are a possibility.

In practice, a vigorous effort to influence a particular government is likely to employ all three approaches, and sometimes the distinctions between them blur. Although even raising such issues as corruption, human rights, or reduced arms outlays can be highly sensitive, persuasion and support are comparatively noncontroversial. The focus of intense debate is the appropriateness and probable effectiveness of various forms of pressure, including conditionality.

VARIETIES OF CONDITIONALITY

The altered international agenda has brought the issue of conditionality front and center. This essay gives special attention to the potential uses, costs, and risks of conditions linked to aid (and in some instances to trade), while keeping in view the broader array of approaches toward the desired goals.

Conditionality entails offering a benefit if and only if the receiver takes specific actions that the donor desires (or refrains from taking actions of which the donor disapproves). Conditionality is usually used to try to bring about durable changes in the recipient's policies and behavior. Generally, those changes are viewed by the donor (and to varying degrees, by the recipient) as intrinsically in the interests of the receiving government, or at least in the interests of the people of the receiving country. The term *conditionality* usually does not refer to the use of aid to purchase actions primarily of importance to the donor, such as base rights or support on a United Nations vote.

Conditionality itself is not a simple concept. The International Monetary Fund and the World Bank (and some bilateral donors) attach rather precise conditions regarding economic reforms to some of their financial assistance, specifying the measures that the recipient must take before funds are released. Both agencies often provide assistance in slices or tranches, with specific conditions required for the release of each tranche. The conditions are tailored to the circumstances of the country, and each case is negotiated separately.

Conditionality can also take the different form of preestablished standards that governments must meet if they are to be eligible for aid. At least in principle, the standards are the same for all potential aid recipients (rather than being tailored to each country). Such standards can be fairly precise and hard: for instance, the European Bank for Reconstruction and Development requires multiparty elections as a precondition for loans. Or the standard can be both vaguer and softer: a statement that the donor will "take into account progress toward improved governance" in determining the level of aid.

In practice, conditionality is always combined with persuasion, and once a government agrees to undertake reforms, financial assistance constitutes direct or indirect support. Conditionality is a more effective approach for some kinds of goals than others: for instance, it works better for goals that can be fairly precisely monitored. The situation in the particular country and the relationship between the donor and recipient also affect how well conditionality works.

Conditionality is resented on three grounds: it is regarded as an invasion of sovereignty; it is an explicit or implicit claim that the donor knows best what is good for the recipient; and it almost always reflects power inequalities. Even if the claims of sovereignty are eroded by the growing consensus on the new international agenda, the second and third sources of resentment will remain. As new conditionalities are introduced—and assuming that older conditionality relating to economic management and reform continues—these inherent strains will intensify. Therefore this essay seeks not only to assess the uses, costs, and risks of conditionality, but also to explore the potential for more consensual alternative approaches to the goals of the new international agenda.

. . . .

THE NEW EMPHASIS ON POLITICAL REFORMS

■   THE THREE MOST DIRECTLY POLITICAL GOALS on the new international agenda are enhanced respect for human rights, improved governance, and democracy. These goals focus on the relations between governments and their citizens. More precisely, they concern the limits of state power vis-à-vis citizens, the functioning of government, and the role of citizens in choosing governments and shaping policy.

Whereas environmental protection and arms reduction in other nations directly affect the security and welfare of the industrial democracies, the political reforms on the new global agenda mainly and directly benefit the people of the nations where the reforms occur. Respect for fundamental human rights has long been viewed as a universal norm. However, the consensus justifying external intervention on behalf of human rights has only gradually evolved, and the scope and limits of that consensus remain unclear. Historically, the United States (as well as some other industrial democracies) has often tried to promote democracy abroad, sometimes by direct political or even military intervention, sometimes more indirectly. Since the Marshall Plan, the rationale for U.S. foreign aid has always included the promotion of democracy. But the dramatic changes of the late 1980s have prompted a surge of interest, in the United States and other industrial democracies, in the more direct and aggressive use of concessional aid to support global democratic trends.

THE EVOLVING CONSENSUS ON THE NEED FOR POLITICAL REFORMS

The idea of basic human rights as a universal norm and an appropriate area for international concern is codified in the Universal Declaration of Human Rights drawn up by the United Nations General Assembly in 1948, and by a series of international charters and agreements ratified since then. These covenants define human rights very broadly. They encompass not only the right to freedom from arbitrary arrest, imprisonment, torture, or "disappearance," but also civil and political rights (including freedom of movement, expression, assembly, and religion) plus a still wider set of economic and social needs (such as employment, shelter, education, and health). Precisely because they are so broad, the covenants are viewed by most governments as statements of long-term aspirations rather than legally binding requirements.

Human rights in the narrowest sense, however, have taken on a special status. Overt and systematic violence by governments against their own citizens prompts universal horror: Nazi Germany, Idi Amin in Uganda, the Khmer Rouge in Cambodia, on a lesser but still tragic scale the military governments of Argentina and Chile, are only some of the instances that come all too readily to mind. The persistent and courageous work of private organizations like Amnesty International has greatly increased recognition of abuses in a great many other nations. The international community is increasingly willing to invoke sanctions against governments that arrest, imprison, torture, or kill their citizens. The end of the Cold War may permit the industrial democracies to pursue this goal more consistently.

The recent emphasis on better governance springs from quite different roots, although it overlaps with human rights concerns. Concern about governance focuses attention not on individual rights but on the institutions and operations of the government, and on the commitment and capacity to govern responsibly and responsively. In part, the recent emphasis on governance grows out of concern over failed economic development in Sub-Saharan Africa. By the late 1980s, both international development agencies and many Africans were pointing to weak, self-serving, and often corrupt governments as perhaps the most serious obstacles to renewed growth.[1] In Latin America as well, persistent fiscal crisis and growing institutional paralysis has prompted intense debate on how to ease the "crisis of the state."

Good governance, like human rights, is interpreted narrowly by some and much more broadly by others. Narrow interpretations focus on increased honesty and efficiency in the public sector and call for heightened attention to public administration and institutional development. But many development specialists note that public administration projects have a mediocre record, in large part because specific improvements in organization, procedures, and technical and managerial training often have little effect in the absence of deeper changes in the political context and the incentives shaping staff behavior.

Broader approaches to governance stress institutions, procedures, and attitudes inside and outside of government that promote openness, accountability, and predictability. For instance, public officials can be held accountable to the public for their actions by subordination to elected officials, direct reporting to and guidance from the legislature, review by a semiautonomous auditing and accounting agency, free media, an autonomous judiciary, active interest associations, outspoken university departments or research institutes, and standards of professional conduct established by specialized associations.

The goal of better governance can also be broadly or narrowly interpreted along a second axis: the range of government activities. In principle, better governance is obviously desirable across the full spectrum of public sector programs and activities. But donors and governments may select more specific areas as particularly crucial: an example might be budgeting and accounting processes. Some donors' recent policy statements expand the term "governance" to cover almost the entire agenda of new global goals. This essay will emphasize "economic governance," referring to increased accountability (not merely more efficient administration) with respect to key economic functions.

Still more recent and somewhat tentative is international agreement that competitive democracy is an appropriate goal worldwide, and furthermore is a legitimate issue for external intervention. This new convention springs from different roots, although it has come to be merged with calls for human rights and improved governance. Many bilateral aid agencies (especially the "like-minded group" including the Scandinavians, the Dutch, and the Canadians) and many nongovernmental organizations have long emphasized extensive participation in development activities by grassroots organizations and middle-level civic associations such as unions. But until quite recently, most donor governments and NGOs alike avoided directly promoting political reforms to encourage increased competition. Such pressure was viewed as a clear invasion of the accepted boundaries of national sovereignty. Moreover, until quite recently, many in industrialized nations questioned whether participatory politics and democratic institutions could be regarded as universal values rather than ethnocentric or culturally specific norms.

The tide of events has largely swept aside such concerns. Earlier hesitations faded as elected governments replaced authoritarian regimes throughout Latin America in the course of the 1980s, while democratic pressures became increasingly clear in Korea, Taiwan, the Philippines, and Pakistan. Events in Eastern Europe in 1989 and 1990, and the surge of democratic initiatives in Sub-Saharan Africa, seemed to definitively establish competitive democracy as a global value. The new prevailing assumption is that specific institutional arrangements will and should vary, but arguments in favor of one-party systems or military governments now sound anachronistic.

Acceptance of competitive democracy as a global norm has also been encouraged by the reversal of older ideas about the relationship between democracy and economic development. During the 1970s and 1980s, many believed that democratic governments' capacity for responsible economic management was handicapped by electoral calculations and popular demands for immediate benefits. The example of the East Asian "tigers" was used to support the argument that authoritarian regimes were more likely to manage their economies to promote growth. By the late 1980s, however, that argument was largely discredited. Analysts comparing economic performance in many countries found no clear evidence of any link between authoritarian or democratic forms of government and either long-term growth or short-term ability to carry out stabilization measures.[2]

Indeed, during the 1980s the conviction spread among donors, in much of the developing world, and also (as we learned later) in many communist nations that perhaps the most formidable obstacle to resumed economic growth is bad governance in the broadest sense: not simply corrupt, incompetent, and overextended government but the repressive political systems that generate such governments. This perception was grafted onto the much older conviction in development circles that widespread participation is a crucial ingredient of economic growth. In short, political liberalization is increasingly regarded as not only consistent with but imperative for sustained economic growth.

This shift in viewpoints is particularly intense and clear in Eastern Europe and Sub-Saharan Africa, where most people believe that past economic failures were inextricably entangled with repressive and nonrepresentative political systems.[3] More generally, all three political objectives—human rights, good governance, and democracy—command support not only in the industrialized democracies but also in most of the less developed world, and in international organizations and private cross-national groups representing their views.

There are of course dissenting views, most obviously from nondemocratic governments, although many of these are also taking some steps toward political liberalization. And even among enthusiastic supporters of the new views, there is considerable disagreement on the extent to which external intervention in the affairs of any nation is warranted to accelerate political reforms. While supporting commitment to democratization, African leaders meeting under the auspices of the Organization for African Unity (OAU) in July 1990 voiced reservations at the prospect of political conditionalities. At the Commonwealth Summit in Harare, Zimbabwe, in October 1991 the governments of India, Malaysia, and Zimbabwe raised similar concerns.[4] Indonesia, confronted with donor indignation over the killing of dozens of unarmed demonstrators in East Timor in late November 1991, emphatically denied that aid should be linked in any way to respect for human rights. Yet others within the poorer nations, particularly political dissidents challenging restrictive governments, favor foreign intervention. They argue that aid has long had the effect (whether or not intended) of propping up dictators. The use of conditioned aid to press for political reform therefore is not new intervention, but intervention turned to more desirable goals.

NEW DONOR POLICIES

Increased consensus regarding political goals has prompted a wave of policy announcements by the industrial democracies. In the two years from late 1989 to late 1991, donor after donor issued statements on the need for political reforms (often as part of larger packages also including reduced expenditures on arms, increased environmental protection, and fresh emphasis on pro-poor strategies). Most of these statements (and the policy guidance that followed the announcements) emphasize dialogue and support as the main approaches, and note the wide array of specific aid activities already supporting human rights, improved governance, and democracy. Beyond these activities, however, almost all of the donors now state that future allocations of aid will reflect recipients' political reforms. Allocative conditionality is the new policy element, and it is therefore a central focus of this essay.

Events in Eastern Europe triggered the shifts. The Group of 24 industrialized nations, set up in mid-1989 to coordinate aid to Poland and Hungary, agreed in late 1989 to extend aid to other East European nations provided that they met free market and political democracy conditions. Accordingly, the charter of the new European Bank for Reconstruction and Development established these criteria as preconditions for assistance.

By 1990 the same principles were being applied (albeit less definitively) to the developing countries in Asia, Latin America, and especially Africa. In January and again in March, French Minister of Cooperation and Development Jacques Pelletier argued that development was not feasible without democracy, and he expressed the hope that African nations would draw inspiration from democratizing trends in Eastern Europe, Latin America, and parts of Asia. France, he stated, would be "very concretely and solidly on the side of those who made, and continue to make, the necessary reforms." President Francois Mitterand emphasized these same themes at a summit at La Boule in June 1990, though he hedged by noting that France would not link aid to specific formal conditions regarding democratic practices.[5]

Similarly, in June 1990, British Foreign Secretary Douglas Hurd argued that increased political freedom and better governance were essential for more satisfactory economic and social progress in Africa. In October he went further. Stating bluntly that "poverty does not justify torture, tyranny, or economic incompetence," he called for a concerted approach by all major aid donors, announced a new British political foundation to assist fledgling political parties, and argued that "we should also look out for opportunities to support countervailing sources of power where it makes sense to do so, along with nongovernmental organizations."[6]

The U.S. Agency for International Development (USAID) followed suit with its "democracy initiative" at the end of 1990. The initiative stated that "within each region of the world, allocations of USAID funds to individual countries will take into account their progress toward democratization," with the objective of placing "democracy on a comparable footing with progress in economic reforms and the establishment of a market-oriented economy, key factors which are already used as criteria for allocating funds." Each of the regional bureaus of USAID are developing their own approach to implementing the initiative. The Latin America bureau plans to use the civil and political rights indices compiled annually by Freedom House as part of its annual allocation process: democratic progress will be accorded a weight of roughly 20 percent (with economic policy performance weighted 50 percent, and social and environmental policies and programs assigned weights of 10 and 20 percent, respectively). The

Africa bureau prefers to develop its own system of evaluation, and plans to focus its assistance substantially on 15 nations selected in part on the basis of performance on governance and democracy criteria.

In Germany, debate throughout 1990 produced new guidelines in 1991, emphasizing political reforms along with reduced expenditures on arms, poverty reduction, and environmental protection. Fairly elaborate evaluation criteria have been developed, but the ministry stresses that application will be flexible and that the criteria themselves are viewed as tentative and likely to evolve.[7] In early 1991, the Netherlands—which has long emphasized poverty reduction and extensive local participation in its aid programs—approved a new policy statement calling for priority for programs to improve observance of human rights, and for countries "that provide grassroots incentives and support."[8] And in April 1991, Japan—now among the largest bilateral aid donors—announced that promotion of democracy, respect for human rights, and reduction of arms production, as well as market-oriented economic policies, will be taken into account in its allocation of aid.[9]

Not only the bilateral aid donors, but also some of the international aid organizations, are giving increased priority to aspects of political reform. The World Bank charter constrains its activities to those promoting economic development. As already noted, it has taken a leading role in arguing that good governance is a crucial ingredient for economic progress, and therefore a legitimate area for its attention. In mid-1991 the executive directors approved a discussion paper on "Managing Development: The Governance Dimension." Like the bilateral donors' policy statements, the World Bank paper emphasizes the importance of dialogue and a variety of specific support activities. However, it adds: "Where dialogue fails, the Bank's own lending to the country is likely to be affected."[10]

As donor after donor announced its intention to direct attention to political reforms, coordination among donors has become an obvious concern. Smaller donors in particular are eager to gain leverage for their own limited programs through concerted action with other donors. In December 1991 the ministerial-level meeting of the Development Assistance Committee (DAC) endorsed "a common approach aimed at promoting human rights and democracy in developing countries," including not only positive measures but also the possibility of deferring or suspending aid in cases of grave violations of human rights. Member states and the Commission of the European Communities agreed to "exchange immediate information . . . and consider joint approaches in reaction to violations." The European Community and its member states also agreed to insert human rights clauses in future cooperation agreements.[11] The donors' consultative groups for specific developing countries, usually chaired by the World Bank, offer another forum for coordination.

ARE THE NEW POLICIES CREDIBLE?

The wave of new policy announcements has been striking. But are donor governments and agencies in fact likely to implement their new priorities? The most skeptical critics suggest that the new policies are at best posturing, and in some cases may be motivated by a desire to camouflage reductions in aid levels or the diversion of assistance from developing nations to Eastern Europe and the fragments of the Soviet Union.

There have already been a few concerted donor responses to political backsliding. Zaire's corrupt and dictatorial government had long been supported by external aid. As Cold War concerns ebbed in 1990, however, Zaire's economic and political performance (already very poor) deteriorated further. Political tensions with Belgium led to sharp cuts in aid, followed by a World Bank decision to reduce its activities to a minimal core program. Other bilateral donors then reduced their aid. The riots of September 1991 led most donors to evacuate their aid missions entirely. Meanwhile, several newly democratic regimes received increased assistance: among these are Namibia, Nepal, and Mongolia, as well as Eastern Europe as a whole.

In Haiti and Kenya, international pressure was more explicitly coordinated. The military coup of September 1991 in Haiti, ousting recently elected President Jean-Bertrand Aristide, prompted unprecedented action by the Organization of American States. Its members agreed to suspend all but humanitarian aid, to impose a trade embargo, and to launch vigorous efforts to mediate an acceptable solution. Deteriorating economic policies and increasing repression of human rights in Kenya prompted members of the World Bank-chaired Consultative Group to suspend new aid pledges for six months in November 1991, pending greater progress on political reform, economic liberalization, and corruption. The action was particularly striking because compared to many other African nations, Kenya's economic policies and performance were not bad, nor was the government more repressive than most of its neighbors. Donors, however, were reacting to deteriorating conditions (including corruption at high levels) coupled with growing popular pressure for political liberalization.

These actions undoubtedly send signals to other governments. However, the signals thus far are distinctly mixed. Donors are reluctant to invoke or sustain sanctions against large and important nations. Most major industrial democracies suspended aid and restricted trade with China after the horrendous Tiananmen Square events of spring 1989. Concerted pressure from the industrial democracies also led the World Bank to suspend most of its activities in China. By 1991, however, most sanctions had been lifted. More recently, responses to Indonesian repression of unarmed demonstrators in late 1991 in Eastern Timor have been minimal.[12]

It is too early to try to assess the new donor policies. However, it seems likely that their impact will fall short of enthusiasts' hopes but will nevertheless help to encourage political reforms. Many of the bilateral donors' recent statements imply that they will gradually shift the allocation of their concessional aid programs to favor those nations making progress on human rights, good governance, and democracy (and sometimes also reduced arms expenditures and environmental protection), while providing reduced or no support to countries that do not improve. The approach is appealing because it is noninterventionist, responding to action in developing nations rather than seeking to prompt or guide sensitive reforms. The reallocation would not occur all at once. But the policy statements do appear to imply that within a few years there would be a distinct relationship between levels of concessional aid in different countries (with appropriate adjustments for population size and poverty levels) and those countries' recent histories of political reform.

In reality, reallocation of concessional aid to favor political reformers and penalize nonreformers is not likely to be so systematic or clear-cut.

Even after several years, the general distribution of concessional aid among countries probably will not closely reflect their record of political reforms. More likely it will be a pattern of ad hoc responses to particularly striking events in specific countries: aid cuts penalizing some (but not all) cases in which internal political behavior is particularly outrageous or serious backsliding occurs, and modest increases in aid for some countries that adopt particularly clear-cut and significant political reforms. The pattern of rewards and punishments will probably be clearer with respect to small and medium-sized countries without major geopolitical importance than for larger and more important aid recipients.

The new policies are likely to lead to ad hoc rather than systematic reallocation for four reasons. With the exception of Japan, total concessional aid levels are probably going to be stable or declining for most donors. Second, reallocation of aid flows in response to recipients' political reforms will be constrained by bilateral donors' conflicting foreign objectives and by the rules of operation in multilateral agencies. Third, donor governments and multilateral agencies are divided and uncertain regarding the priority to accord the new objectives. Fourth, political reforms are complex; countries may make progress on some aspects and lose ground on others. Therefore, donors may find it difficult to gauge whether a country has improved or deteriorated, and still harder to compare its performance to that of other nations. The first three reasons are discussed below; the fourth is explored later in this essay.

AID LEVELS. Some donors claim to have increased support and set aside specific funds or targets for activities directly related to human rights, good governance, and democracy. In fiscal year 1990, USAID allocated roughly $100 million for democracy and human rights projects.[13] That figure is expected to increase substantially in fiscal years 1991 and 1992. In June 1991, the Overseas Development Administration (ODA) of the United Kingdom announced a target of $50 million to be committed to assistance for improved governance and the development of democratic and pluralistic structures in the coming year.[14] However, in neither USAID nor ODA are these sums additive. Rather, aspects of ongoing programs are being attributed to the new initiatives. In USAID the sum is not a result of a centrally established target, but rather results from adding up ongoing and new projects in individual country missions.

More generally, most donors are not likely to increase their concessional flows to developing nations in the next few years. In the United States, a systematic winding down of old Cold War activities could free substantial funds for new initiatives without increasing overall expenditures on foreign affairs.[15] Currently, however, a little under half of U.S. bilateral economic aid remains committed to Egypt and Israel, and allocations of the balance are constrained by a mind-numbing array of legislative earmarks and restrictions. Public (and therefore congressional) opinion is also likely to balk at significant increases in foreign aid, perhaps with some modest exception for Eastern Europe and the republics of the Soviet Union.

U.S. ability to reward political reforms is therefore limited. For example, the U.S. government sought to support recent economic and political reforms in Ethiopia with a modest $60 million for economic and democracy projects. But Ethiopia is in arrears on payment of debts incurred in the 1970s, and new U.S. aid is blocked under the terms of the Brooke amendment. An attempt by the State Department and Congress to provide a one-year waiver for Ethiopia was frustrated since the provision was attached to the defeated 1992 foreign aid bills.[16]

Most other donors do not have much greater flexibility. Germany has mounted ambitious aid efforts in Eastern Europe and the Soviet Union.[17] Those flows, plus the extraordinary costs of integrating East Germany and the expenses associated with the further integration of the European Community, will almost surely rule out sizable increases to other regions of the world. The challenges of European integration, the effort to provide some assistance to the former communist states, and perhaps the dwindling of some traditional commercial and foreign policy interests in Africa are likely to similarly constrain France. Nor are higher foreign aid budgets anticipated in the United Kingdom or most of the smaller donors. Japan alone among the bilateral donors is likely to increase its economic assistance significantly during the 1990s. Ironically, much of Japan's aid is concentrated in Asia, where the consensus regarding global political norms is weakest.

CONFLICTING FOREIGN OBJECTIVES. In the past, industrial nations' dedication to promoting political reform abroad has almost always been subordinated to other foreign policy goals. The pattern is particularly well illustrated by the history of U.S. human rights policy, briefly reviewed later in this essay. As already noted, the fading of Cold War concerns has increased the priority of goals such as human rights, improved governance, and democracy. Some other foreign policy concerns are also dwindling, leaving more scope to pursue the new global values. Security issues in Central America are now greatly diminished, while the long impasses in Southern Africa, Cambodia, and even North Korea now offer varying degrees of promise for resolution. Historic relationships and sensitivities between patron and client nations that used to influence aid allocation patterns are also receding into the past. The roles of the United Kingdom, France, and Belgium in Africa are now less shaped by former colonial ties than was true in 1960 or even 1980. Similarly, the special relationships between the United States and Liberia, and the United States and the Philippines, have clearly eroded.

But other foreign policy concerns, of course, continue to be salient. Where these conflict with the new political reform goals, the former are likely to dominate. Security concerns remain overriding in the Middle East, intermingled with the politics of oil. The emergence of independent Islamic-majority states along the southern tier of the former Soviet Union heightens security concerns in the Islamic crescent stretching from Pakistan to Morocco. Tensions between India and its neighbors continue to be major issues in South Asia. Conflict between Russia and its neighbors or between other adjacent republics may turn out to be a key concern in the territory of the Soviet Union.

Commercial and financial interests will rise higher on the foreign policy agendas of the industrial democracies in a world they now find less threatening militarily. Increasing trade competition and new regional blocs will probably intensify such pressures. Major trade or investment interests are likely to prevail over policies to promote political reforms abroad. For instance, business interests in both Japan and the United States have played a major role in loosening trade sanctions imposed on China after the Tiananmen Square massacre and prompting the resumption of Japanese aid flows.

BUREAUCRATIC CONSTRAINTS. In addition to competition from other foreign policy goals, bureaucratic rivalries and resistance within donor governments predictably will hamper consistent implementation of the new policies. As a general rule, country officers in ministries of foreign affairs as well as aid agencies resent general policy directives that restrict their flexibility. Moreover, not all aid agency staff share the new perspective that political reforms are crucial to promote economic and social development. Many would prefer to focus on more traditional development tasks and believe that these may be endangered by the new initiatives. In the international financial institutions, this reaction is reinforced by the nature of their charters. "Initiative fatigue" is also a factor older aid officials in a number of donor governments have seen reorientations and new initiatives come and go every few years for the past three decades.

The vigor and consistency of the new policies will also be affected by interagency perspectives and rivalries within donor governments. In some cases, foreign ministries are more enthusiastic than aid agencies, in others less. Decisionmaking authority is often divided or shared among agencies. For instance, the U.S. State Department largely determines the allocation of economic support funds, comprising roughly 40 percent of U.S. bilateral economic assistance, while USAID has much fuller control over development assistance funds. The Departments of Treasury, Agriculture, and Commerce also have some voice in certain decisions, but relatively little concern for the new goals. In France, project and budget support loans to African and some other developing nations are channeled through the Caisse Centrale de Cooperation Economique, which is controlled by the Direction du Tresor. The very extensive technical assistance programs are implemented through several separate agencies; and both the Foreign Ministry and the Elysée (the office of the president) have considerable voice in many decisions. Commitment to the new agenda varies sharply among these agencies. In Germany, the Foreign Ministry and the Ministry of Development Cooperation have quite different perspectives on global political goals. Divergent views also will affect how vigorously the World Bank pursues better governance: executive board directors representing industrial democracies are likely to press for more vigorous implementation than those representing developing nations.

Taking into account competing objectives, limited aid budgets, and bureaucratic constraints on implementation, political reforms clearly will not become the primary concern determining the allocation of the industrialized democracies' concessional aid to poorer nations. But the new goals may play a considerably larger role than they have in the past. They will continue to have high priority in the aid programs of the Scandinavians and the Dutch. All donors will tend to pursue political reforms most vigorously in small and poor countries that depend heavily on foreign aid. And for the first time, the new global goals will become part of the agenda for coordinated policy and action by donors.

Therefore, the vigorous discussions and debates among donors and between donors and recipients regarding how external actors can best promote these goals are neither posturing nor visionary. The role of conditionality as a specific means to encourage political reforms remains unclear, however, and may well turn out to be both less important and different in nature from what recent policy statements imply. Allocative conditionality—distributing aid in accord with progress toward political goals—is likely to be less a systematic and consistent strategy than an ad hoc response to particular events in specific nations. A strategy of strict allocative conditionality raises many questions. What are the criteria for gauging the level and trends of human rights protection, good governance, and democracy? If some aspects of a government's performance are improving while others are not (or may even be slipping backward), which aspects are most important? Should standard criteria be used for all recipients, or should each country be judged solely against its own past record? A less consistent ad hoc pattern of conditionality finesses these questions, but raises others. If a major step forward (for instance, fair elections) is rewarded with significantly increased aid, is that likely to reduce leverage on other reforms (political or economic) that remain to be addressed? If political backsliding is penalized by reducing aid, is influence increased or diminished?

Moreover, the distinction between general criteria used in allocating aid and specific conditions applied to particular governments is likely to break down in practice. An aid-dependent government under strong donor pressure (especially coordinated pressure from all donors) is likely to ask, openly or privately, "What must we do to satisfy you?" The answer

(for example: release the political prisoners incarcerated in the past several months; remove constraints on opposition newspapers; schedule elections within a reasonable period) amounts to specific conditionality.
Depending on the nature of the specific conditions and on the strength of
reform sentiment within the government itself, implementation of the conditions will then raise a variety of issues similar to those involved in
prompting economic reforms.

Aid donors are currently feeling their way regarding how to use
conditionality to promote their new agendas. A review of past experience
with aid conditionality can suggest some relevant lessons.

. . . .

LESSONS FROM EXPERIENCE

■   DURING THE TWENTIETH CENTURY, the United States has tried
to promote democracy abroad on many occasions and through many
means, direct and indirect, massive and modest. So too have other
wealthy democratic nations, in varying degrees. The roster of attempts
ranges from military threats or invasions to quiet ambassadorial advice,
from large-scale economic assistance to low-key efforts to encourage
grassroots participation, from trade sanctions or concessions to monitoring elections. Given the scope and variety of efforts, it is perhaps not sur-
prising that different analysts reach contrary conclusions regarding their
effectiveness. For instance, Abraham Lowenthal and 14 other scholars
examined American efforts to encourage democracy in Latin America
during the twentieth century. Lowenthal concludes that U.S. efforts,
although often sincere, were sporadic and limited; moreover, the "U.S.
drive to export democracy has only rarely had a positive and lasting
impact." Samuel P. Huntington, on the other hand, surveying the wave of
transitions from authoritarian to more democratic governments since the
early 1970s, concludes that America's role was "critical" in 10 countries
and an important "contributing factor" in six others.[18]

This essay focuses on a much narrower issue: the uses and limits
of conditions attached to foreign economic and security assistance as a
means of encouraging political reforms. Even this topic offers a wider

range of experience than can be reviewed here. Perhaps the most instructive aspect of U.S. experience with political conditionality is the effort since the mid-1970s to link aid to respect for human rights. The experience of the World Bank and the International Monetary Fund in requiring specific policy reforms offers still more valuable lessons, because their conditions are much more extensive and consistently applied. Even though their influence has focused on economic reforms, the lessons can be easily transferred to problems of political reform.

U.S. HUMAN RIGHTS EXPERIENCE

LEGAL PROVISIONS. For nearly two decades policymakers have incorporated broad human rights concerns into U.S. bilateral and multilateral policy and foreign aid allocations. Beginning in 1973, an extensive series of hearings under the leadership of Representative Donald M. Fraser (D-Minn.), then the chairman of the House Subcommittee on International Organizations and Movements, brought the human rights conditions of U.S. aid recipients into the public eye. Since that time, human rights concerns have held a permanent and often contentious place on the U.S. foreign policy agenda.

Three pieces of general legislation initiated by Congress in the 1970s form the cornerstones of U.S. human rights policy. They aim to guide U.S. policy in allocating economic and military assistance and in voting at the international financial institutions. The notion that human rights should be considered when providing military assistance was first offered as a "sense of the Congress" resolution in 1974. The linkage was made legally binding in 1978 with an amendment to Section 502B of the Foreign Assistance Act of 1961, which prohibited security assistance to "any country the government of which engages in a consistent pattern of gross violations of internationally recognized human rights." The ban on security assistance includes direct military aid, commercial arms sales, military education and training, antiterrorism assistance, and economic support funds (ESF). The law also includes an escape clause that allows the president to determine that "extraordinary circumstances exist warranting provision of such assistance."[19]

Just as members of Congress feared that U.S. military assistance might contribute directly to human rights violations, they reasoned that promoting economic growth with U.S. economic assistance might reward repressive regimes and perhaps encourage further repression. In 1975, Congress passed mandatory legislation to condition economic aid on respect for human rights with Section 116 of the Foreign Assistance Act of 1961, also known as the Harkin amendment after its sponsor, Representative Tom Harkin (D-Iowa).

No assistance may be provided under this provision to the government of any country that engages in a consistent pattern of gross violations of internationally recognized human rights, including torture or cruel, inhuman, or degrading treatment or punishment, prolonged detention without charges, causing the disappearance of persons by the abduction and clandestine detention of those persons, or other flagrant denial of the right of life, liberty, and the security of persons unless such assistance will directly benefit the needy people in such country.[20]

The U.S. legislation, then, focused on human rights defined as security of the person, though broader civil and political rights are also considered in U.S. policy. The legislation emphasized negative conditionality, that is, punishment of human rights abusers. However, Section 116(e) authorized a more positive approach, permitting funds to be used for the promotion of civil and political rights. The conditions of Section 116 were subsequently applied to the Food for Peace Program (P.L. 480) and to insurance provided through the Overseas Private Investment Corporation.

After much debate, a third human rights provision was enacted to influence the flow of multilateral aid through such institutions as the World Bank and the Inter-American Development Bank. Specifically, Section 701 of the International Financial Assistance Act of 1977 instructs the U.S. government, by means of its voice and vote in the multilateral development banks, "to advance the cause of human rights, including by seeking to channel assistance toward countries other than those whose governments engage in gross violations of internationally recognized human rights." Human rights concerns were also loosely linked to U.S. policy at the Export-Import Bank in legislation that was later repealed.[21]

In addition to these three laws guiding direct and indirect U.S. foreign assistance, U.S. trade has legally been linked—though more narrowly—to human rights. The Jackson-Vanik amendment to the Trade Act of 1974 prohibits granting most-favored-nation (MFN) status and credit to any country that denies its citizens the right to emigrate. The amendment was created with Soviet Jews in mind but was used as a springboard for general discussions on human rights and trade with Eastern Europe and the Soviet Union throughout the 1970s and 1980s.[22]

PROBLEMS OF IMPLEMENTATION. Implementation of these laws by the executive branch has varied sharply under different presidents. Even before his election, Jimmy Carter promised to make the issue of human rights a high priority in his administration. In his first year, he cut off security assistance to Argentina, Bolivia, El Salvador, Guatemala, Haiti, Nicaragua, Paraguay, and Uruguay on human rights grounds. He created the interagency Christopher Committee to ensure that human rights were taken into account at all levels of the government. Rhetorically, Carter even endorsed the concept of socioeconomic rights. In practice, however, Carter's policy has been criticized for being inconsistent. For geopolitical reasons, human rights violations seemed to go unnoticed in the Philippines, South Korea, Iran, and Zaire.[23]

As a presidential candidate, Ronald Reagan strongly criticized Carter's human rights policy, accusing him of weakening the U.S. position in the Cold War by being too critical of strategic allies. International terrorism—defined as communism—would replace human rights as a priority. Reagan's philosophy was articulated in a particularly influential article by scholar Jeane Kirkpatrick on "Dictatorships and Double Standards," in which she rationalized that human rights violations by totalitarian communist regimes were worse than those of authoritarian dictatorships.[24] No security assistance was terminated on human rights grounds during Reagan's first term. On the contrary, he restored assistance to Argentina, Chile, Guatemala, and Uruguay. During his second term, Reagan seemed to accord somewhat higher priority to human rights policy in some cases. In several, such as Chile and the Philippines, domestic and foreign public pressure or political events within the countries may well have prompted this apparent shift.[25]

Even under the Carter administration, however, Congress and the executive branch battled over how to implement the general human rights legislation. The presidential office fought to maintain its executive prerogative to formulate foreign policy, Congress fought to uphold the spirit and letter of its own laws. Although Section 502B has never been formally invoked, it has provided the foundation for Congress to pressure the executive branch regarding security assistance and human rights. When Congress felt that the executive branch was not carrying out its intent, it passed country-specific legislation restricting U.S. assistance according to the particular circumstances of a recipient country. Often such legislation was the result of extensive congressional hearings and took the form of amendments to foreign aid bills. In recent years, Congress has used country-specific legislation to cease security assistance to El Salvador, Guatemala, Haiti, Liberia, and Somalia, among others.[26]

Human rights concerns also created conflicts among and within various executive branch agencies. The State Department's Bureau of Human Rights and Humanitarian Affairs, created by Congress in 1974, often found its efforts blocked by the regional bureaus interested in maintaining friendly relations with their respective countries. Similarly, the Departments of Treasury and Commerce opposed human rights actions that threatened the economic and business interests for which they are responsible.[27] These many tensions contributed to the inconsistent record of U.S. human rights policy.

The case of El Salvador is a highly publicized and vivid example of the conflict between Congress and the executive branch, and the weakness of the U.S. effort to encourage human rights when the effort conflicted with other foreign policy goals. In the early 1980s, Congress passed a law cutting military aid to El Salvador, but included a loophole allowing aid to continue if the president certified that the human rights situation was improving. From January 1981 to July 1983, President Reagan signed the certification every six months—during the most extreme repression in El Salvador's history. At the time of the execution of six Jesuit priests and two witnesses in 1990, the United States had provided almost $1 billion in military assistance to a country with a population of 5 million. Congress cut military aid to El Salvador in half in late 1989, but President Bush restored full funding in 1991.[28]

For most developing countries, the international financial institutions are a greater source of capital than U.S. bilateral aid. U.S. policymakers are generally reluctant to "politicize" these economic institutions with issues such as human rights. The record of implementing Section 701 at the multilateral development banks (MDBs) changed sharply under different administrations. During Carter's term, the United States refused support for 118 loans for 16 countries on human rights grounds. However, U.S. representatives in the MDBs are responsible to the Treasury and not the State Department or USAID. In the World Bank, they made little effort to influence other donors' stances, and most of the loans were approved over pro forma U.S. objections. The Reagan administration aggressively reversed Carter's policy, and during its first few months in office approved loans for Argentina, Chile, Paraguay, and Uruguay. Under the Bush administration, U.S. Executive Directors to the World Bank have abstained from voting based on the human rights records of applicants, though not consistently.[29]

In 1991, links between trade preferences and human rights became the center of intense debate between the chief executive and Congress. In accord with his explicit opposition to all conditions and his belief that "engagement" with China would provide greater leverage than would disengagement, President Bush announced he would renew MFN status for China. Many members of Congress, however, felt that the Chinese government had never been properly reprimanded for the massacre at Tiananmen Square. Legislation that would revoke MFN on human rights grounds was introduced, and both bodies of Congress eventually passed a bill placing conditions on the MFN renewal, including the release of prisoners arrested for prodemocracy protests and the halt of exports to the United States produced by forced labor. President Bush vetoed the measure in March 1992 and congressional support is likely to fall short of the votes needed to override the veto.

LESSONS FROM U.S. HUMAN RIGHTS POLICY. U.S. experience with linking aid to respect for human rights underscores the points made earlier in this essay. First, human rights objectives (and probably other political reform goals) must compete with and are likely to be subordinated to national security and other foreign policy concerns. The U.S. government was more willing to confront an aid recipient about its human rights violations if that country was not a strategic player in the Cold War.

Similarly, the United States was more willing to take issue with smaller countries, or aid recipients without significant economic importance to the United States. Thus we see action taken against countries such as Paraguay and Uruguay, but not countries such as Iran, the Philippines, and South Korea. The deteriorating Soviet threat does not automatically give human rights much higher priority. The 1991 Human Rights Watch report recently accused the Bush administration of subordinating human rights concerns to trade interests with China, fighting the drug war in Peru, and remaining friendly with oil-producing states in the Middle East.[30]

Inconsistent and uncoordinated implementation is a second and closely related theme in the history of U.S. human rights policy, with obvious relevance for future efforts. The case of Argentina provides an example. In the late 1970s, the U.S. government ceased military supply and training, abstained from voting on Argentine loans at the World Bank, and used diplomatic channels to pressure the Argentine government on human rights. These integrated efforts sent a clear message to Argentina of the strong U.S. commitment to human rights. U.S. officials eased their pressure, however, after the Soviet invasion of Afghanistan, because they hoped to convince Argentina to join the grain embargo against the Soviet Union.[31] When President Reagan took office, he restored security assistance and began voting in favor of Argentine loans at the international financial institutions. Persistent tensions between Congress and the chief executive, and among government agencies, also undercut the effectiveness of the U.S. human rights policy.[32]

If the difficulties and failures of U.S. experience with conditioning aid on respect for human rights counsel caution regarding more ambitious political conditionality, the achievements of past policy are also important to note. Over the longer run, the policy of conditionality is one of many influences that has contributed to significant progress in the area of human rights. Among these positive effects is the heightened awareness of human rights concerns. Although the consistency of President Carter's human rights policy has been questioned, his personal commitment and concern for the victims of human rights violations was indubitable. The language of human rights became incorporated into official statements and front-page newspaper reporting from around the world. And interest in human rights continues to swell: Amnesty International currently boasts a grassroots membership of more than 1 million people in over 150 countries.[33]

Closely related is the dramatic improvement in human rights monitoring over the past two decades. Along with the human rights legislation in the mid-1970s, Congress mandated that the State Department's Bureau of Human Rights and Humanitarian Affairs produce annual reports on the human rights conditions of every country in the United Nations. Nongovernmental human rights organizations, highly critical of the bureau's "Country Reports on Human Rights Practices" in the early years, acknowledge that the reporting has steadily improved. This is largely a result of better training for foreign service officers around the world who are now required to investigate and report on human rights conditions.[34] Combined with the important work of groups such as Amnesty International and Human Rights Watch, policymakers have current, extensive information available at all times when making foreign aid—and other foreign policy—decisions.

The U.S. experience with using conditionality to encourage human rights has mainly relied on the negative approach of denying aid or threatening to deny aid as a punishment to abusers. On the positive side, Section 116 of the Foreign Assistance Act does authorize a small amount of money to help recipient countries develop institutions to promote human rights, as long as the support does not influence an election or support a political party in any way. The United States also donates funds to the International Committee of the Red Cross and OAS Inter-American Commission on Human Rights. Both donors and recipients have expressed interest in further developing methods of "positive conditionality" in which governments would be rewarded for improvements in human rights.

Other industrialized democracies followed the U.S. lead in officially linking aid to human rights. Several broadened the U.S. definition of human rights to include economic and social rights. The Netherlands, Norway, and Canada, in particular, consider the human rights policy of recipient countries among the criteria for receiving aid and emphasize a more positive approach of providing aid to help promote the conditions that foster the observance of human rights. At various times, each donor government has also employed a more punitive conditionality on human rights grounds: the Netherlands cut aid to Suriname in 1982; Norway withdrew aid to Chile in 1974 and to Sri Lanka in 1987; Canada reduced aid to Uganda in the 1970s, and to El Salvador and Guatemala during the 1980s, among others.[35]

IMF AND WORLD BANK EXPERIENCE WITH ECONOMIC CONDITIONALITY

WHY WORLD BANK AND IMF ECONOMIC CONDITIONALITY IS RELEVANT. Since the International Monetary Fund (IMF) began operations in 1946, it has provided loans accompanied with policy conditions to help member governments correct balance-of-payments deficits and contain inflation. The World Bank, with a much broader mandate to promote economic development, operated largely through project aid until 1980. Convinced that inappropriate economic policies were the main cause of flagging growth, above all in Sub-Saharan Africa, the World Bank then began experimenting with nonproject aid conditioned on specific economic reforms. By 1989, "policy-based" loans accounted for 30 percent of World Bank assistance, and more than 60 countries had received one or more such loans. The ratio of policy-based to total lending dropped to 19 percent in 1970.[36] Although the specific reforms required are quite different from the political reforms we have been considering, the record of what has worked and what has failed, and why, is relevant for political as well as economic reforms.

Moreover, IMF and World Bank experience with conditions can be viewed as a rough gauge of the maximum potential of the approach. In contrast to U.S. experience with respect to human rights, the Bretton Woods organizations are largely free to pursue their mandated goals without being constrained by conflicting objectives. The United States and other major industrial powers only rarely use their influence to inject political considerations into lending projects. While interagency and interbranch rivalries and disagreements handicapped U.S. human rights policy, the World Bank and especially the IMF are comparatively tightly disciplined and unitary organizations. Their leverage is presumably high: IMF high-conditionality loans only come into play when a government is in severe difficulties, and the World Bank during the 1980s was a major source of financial aid for a great many hard-pressed nations. This leverage was enhanced because many bilateral donors oriented parts of their assistance to the leadership of the IMF and the World Bank, as did the commercial banks with respect to debt relief. Both organizations have staffs well respected for their expertise. All these considerations should facilitate the effective use of conditionality.

COMPLIANCE WITH ECONOMIC REFORM CONDITIONS. According to the organizations' assessments, compliance with IMF and World Bank conditions is quite high. (As discussed below, however, compliance can be a quite misleading gauge for real influence). Eighty-five percent of IMF standby and extended arrangements approved by the executive board between 1983 and 1990 continued in effect until completion; many, though not all, of the remainder were terminated because the government failed to comply with agreed conditions. A second analysis of agreements in effect during 1985-88 concluded that compliance with different types of performance targets ranged from roughly 65 to 80 percent.[37] World Bank assessments of its experience with policy-based lending during the 1980s concluded that about two-thirds of all legally binding conditions were fully implemented during the lifetime of the loan; an additional 18 percent were substantially fulfilled. The compliance rate was higher for more recent loans.[38]

These assessments of compliance may be biased upward, and should certainly be viewed with some caution. The World Bank's quantitative "scores" are based on qualitative judgments of compliance with thousands of conditions, assessed initially by junior researchers, with some second reviews and quality controls built into the process. The conditions themselves were often fairly loosely drawn, and still more loosely interpreted in the actual management of the loans. The impression of precise measurement is surely misleading, and experienced reviewers of the record might well arrive at considerably less hopeful conclusions.[39] Some still more fundamental questions regarding the real meaning of compliance are considered a little later.

More interesting (and probably more reliable) than measurement of overall compliance levels is the evidence, from the IMF and still more clearly the World Bank assessments, that compliance varies substantially depending on the type of policy reform being encouraged. A number of generalizations grow out of their experience:

- Compliance rates are highest for those measures that can be put into effect by a small number of central government officials and readily monitored by available indicators. Such measures include reforms in price, interest, and exchange-rate policies, as well as credit ceilings. Most IMF conditions, and a smaller proportion of World Bank conditions, focus on such actions.

- Compliance is likely to be better for reforms supported by a strong technical consensus such as macroeconomic stabilization measures. Conditionality is inappropriate and likely to be ineffective when it is used to press for measures lacking a technical consensus, such as in many aspects of agricultural policy.[40]

- Compliance tends to be high for "single shot" measures (such as devaluation) in contrast to reforms that require an extended series of decisions and actions. Relatedly, conditions can be particularly useful if they focus on measures that break bottlenecks, that is, steps that set in train a series of further actions by the government or private firms or groups that lock in the reform.

Conversely, compliance with conditions tends to be less likely and conditions are often inappropriate for reforms with the following characteristics:

- Reforms requiring extensive institutional change tend to produce low compliance. Some conditions that are politically popular, like improved export financing, may be poorly implemented because they entail complex institutional change.[41] Institutional changes are much harder to monitor objectively than are price changes. They are inherently more complex and require extensive follow-up decisions.

- Compliance is also likely to be weak where reforms require the cooperation of many agencies, in contrast to decisions that can be made and executed by a handful of key economic officials. The inducement offered by the conditional aid is likely to be irrelevant to at least some of the key groups needed to implement the reform. The minister of finance or the governor of the central bank bears direct responsibility for a gaping fiscal deficit or accelerating inflation. A sizable nonproject loan or grant directly eases their burden and provides a major inducement for them to undertake reforms directly under their control. In contrast, consider a structural adjustment loan requiring a fundamental overhaul of a major state economic enterprise. The reform requires cooperation from both management and workers, but neither will receive any direct gain from the loan; on the contrary, their security and status are severely threatened.

■ Compliance may also be weak if a reform requires cooperation or responses from the private sector. For instance, privatization of government economic enterprises requires private parties willing to bid.[42]

The fundamental logic underlying these points applies as much to political as to economic reforms. A condition requiring the release of political prisoners can be carried out by a decision of top political leaders: conditionality might be appropriate. But if human rights are being widely violated by dozens of largely autonomous vigilante groups, bands of marauding soldiers, or warring ethnic groups, central government officials may well lack the power to contain them. In such cases conditionality is probably futile. Another example: specific legislation or regulations muzzling the press or hobbling the formation of unions and civic associations might be an appropriate target for conditionality. Such reforms can often be revised by a few key officials, and it is easy to monitor whether they have been changed. In contrast, conditionality is probably not a useful way to press central government agencies to consult with local citizens' committees on local projects. Implementing such a condition requires extensive institutional innovation and sensitivity and commitment on the part of central and local officials. It also requires cooperation from local citizens. Such requirements are not created by decree nor are they easy to monitor objectively.

COMPLIANCE, COMMITMENT, AND REAL INFLUENCE. World Bank and IMF experience with pressing economic reforms demonstrates that the effectiveness of conditionality varies not only with different types of reforms, but also with different circumstances in the recipient country.

First and quite obviously, conditionality is more effective if governments are highly dependent on aid. Compliance is less likely if a government knows or thinks that it has recourse to alternative resources.

During much of the 1980s, for example, Brazilian foreign exchange reserves were strong as a result of booming exports. External donors' leverage was correspondingly limited and very little conditional lending was attempted, even though the economy badly needed a wide range of reforms. Compliance with conditions requiring economic reforms also reflects the degree to which the government actually believes in or "owns" the reforms. The point is obvious, but raises several fundamental issues regarding the real effects of conditionality.

A government may meet many or all of the legal conditions for a loan and the additional "understandings" that are part of the supporting documentation (though not legally binding), yet may undercut the objectives of these requirements by failing to take still other supplementary or follow-up actions. If powerful groups within the government oppose the reforms, they may even directly take countervailing measures, while complying with the formal conditions for the loan.

Indeed, where governments are not committed to reforms but badly need external finance, and where donors feel under some obligation to provide funds, the process of conditionality can degenerate into a charade. Without ownership, extensive use of conditions is likely to produce elaborate games of superficial or partial compliance, failure to adopt key supplementary measures to make the reforms effective, or a trail of reform efforts launched and abandoned. These games are worse than frustrating; they destroy the credibility of the reform process within the country concerned, and they obstruct dialogue and persuasion between the government and external donors or creditors.[43]

Even where compliance with conditions is paralleled by the broader thrust of government actions, it is not clear whether the conditions actually caused the policy reforms. One expects the fullest compliance from governments already largely committed to reforms. In such cases, however, the government would probably have pursued similar reforms without the conditions—although the financial support may well accelerate or broaden reform decisions and facilitate implementation. High compliance, in short, does not necessarily imply strong influence.

Conversely, poor compliance does not necessarily imply lack of influence. Even failed conditions may push some officials and groups to consider seriously options that had not before been on the policy agenda.

In the course of the 1980s, ideas regarding appropriate economic policies and strategies changed radically in many developing nations. Conditionality probably contributed to the process of rethinking old assumptions in some cases, even where the conditions themselves were resented and may have been implemented only partially or not at all.

Just as experience with promoting different categories of economic reforms applied quite readily to political reforms, so these basic points regarding the effects of aid dependence and of governmental commitment also bear on political conditionality. Political conditions linked to aid are likely to have little or no effect in countries in which the need for aid is marginal. And if the government is reluctant to make required changes, the potential for halfhearted or sham compliance is obvious. But, as with economic conditions, political conditions may sometimes focus and accelerate debate and rethinking within the recipient government and country, pushing people to consider options they had not seriously weighed before. In the 1990s, a reassessment is under way in much of the world regarding the role of governments and their relations with their citizens. As with the economic reassessments of the 1980s, conditionality, directed to political rather than economic reforms, may well contribute to the rethinking process.

In sum, experience makes clear that conditions attached to aid can effectively promote certain types of reforms, if the donor is prepared to enforce the conditions more or less consistently, and if the recipient needs the assistance. However, conditionality also carries costs and risks. Used too much or for the wrong goals, it can divert attention from substantive issues to procedure and bargaining; it can discredit necessary measures by making them appear imposed from without; or it can undermine officials' sense of responsibility for their own actions and their country's fate. Extensive use of conditionality also carries costs for the donor: it consumes a great deal of staff time and energy, may sour the atmosphere for dialogue, and can create painful dilemmas pitting credibility against realistic flexibility. The potential gains from using conditions to promote important political objectives need to be weighed, in each situation, against the costs, and against the prospects for achieving desired reforms by other means. The next two sections explore some of these issues with respect to each main category of political reforms over a range of country circumstances.

. . . .

CONDITIONAL AID AS A MEANS FOR ADVANCING DIFFERENT POLITICAL REFORMS

■ SOME OF THE RECENT policy statements on political reforms imply or state that respect for human rights, improved governance, and democracy form a seamless web: advancing one goal will advance the others. Moreover, new donor policies often present political reforms as part of a package including other goals as well: environmental protection, promotion of the welfare of the poor, and reduction in arms expenditures. Sometimes the term "good governance" is used very broadly to encompass all of these goals.[44]

The three sets of political goals do indeed overlap and support each other in many ways. Basic personal security from arbitrary government abuse is a vital underpinning for both good economic governance and pluralistic politics. The links are many: to note only two, a fairly free press and an independent and competent judiciary are important safeguards for good governance as well as crucial for democracy. Yet it is equally clear that the three sets of goals do not always go together. Consider the following points.

Under certain kinds of strain, even firmly democratic governments may compromise human rights. Ethnic separatists, ideologically motivated guerrillas or terrorists, and drug rings all pose threats likely to prompt human rights abuses: democratic Sri Lanka's serious violations in the course of combating ethnic separatists are one example among many.

Moreover, in countries with pervasive ethnic or regional tensions, freer political competition is likely to provoke conflict or even disintegration: witness events in Yugoslavia and the Soviet Union. Ethnic strife was one of the key rationales for abandoning competitive party systems in Africa in the 1960s. In Nigeria over the past several years, the military government has sought to engineer a return to democratic institutions that will not rekindle ethnic conflict; to that end, it has imposed constraints on the number and nature of political parties.

Democracy and good economic governance are substantially independent of each other. In the 1970s and most of the 1980s, Chile under Pinochet, Korea, Taiwan, and Singapore met most of the criteria of good economic governance, but they were hardly democratic. Chile, and to a lesser degree the others, combined good economic governance with serious violations of basic human rights. Conversely, a number of established democracies have serious problems with corruption and administrative incompetence. Moreover, the history of most established democracies suggests that building and maintaining competitive political parties usually involves patronage and clientelism, entailing some compromises with standards of good governance.

Political reforms are currently being urged not only because they are intrinsically desirable, but because they help to establish an environment conducive to economic growth. But there is no general relationship between democratic or authoritarian forms of government and economic growth. Some authoritarian governments (especially in Asia) have promoted impressive growth. Others (especially in Africa) have virtually wrecked their countries' economies. Some democratic governments have excellent records of economic reform and growth; others have done poorly.

In the 1990s, an unprecedented number of countries are seeking to move simultaneously from authoritarian to more open polities, and from state-guided to more open economies. Though pluralist politics and market economies are probably mutually essential in the long run, the processes of moving toward each goal conflict in many ways in the short and medium run. Among many probable tensions: recently empowered working- and middle-class groups will oppose dismantling consumer subsidies (and also the indirect subsidies for state enterprises that sustained many of their jobs), yet the subsidies are major causes of economic distortions and decline.[45]

In short, all good things do not automatically go together. We cannot comfortably assume that various political reforms will necessarily complement each other or be consistent with other high-priority objectives. The linkages are complex and vary with specific circumstances.

These caveats are certainly not an argument against measures to promote stronger human rights observance, better governance, broadened participation, or freer political contestation. But they underscore some fundamental facts to keep in mind as we consider *how* to promote these goals. More specifically, these considerations, coupled with the lessons from the past with conditionality, counsel caution and point toward different roles for conditionality with respect to each broad category of political reform.

CONDITIONALITY AND BETTER ECONOMIC GOVERNANCE

The international consensus on human rights rests on moral concerns. The growing consensus on the importance of good economic governance, in contrast, rests on the pragmatic judgment that in its absence, economic development is crippled and foreign aid is largely wasted.

The criteria for good economic governance are less precise than those defining human rights violations (narrowly defined), and there is no organization pursuing "Integrity International" analogous to Amnesty International and its sister organizations monitoring human rights.[46] However, techniques could certainly be developed for assessing certain standard aspects at the core of accountability, transparency, and predictability. Because improved economic governance is directly and inextricably linked to economic growth, major aid donors have an obvious pragmatic rationale for requiring reform. Conditionality for improved economic governance is really an extension of economic policy conditionality and is likely to take the same specific forms.

CONDITIONALITY AND HUMAN RIGHTS

Among the political goals on the new global agenda, human rights, defined fairly narrowly as the right to freedom from arbitrary arrest, imprisonment, torture, and "disappearance," clearly commands the most intense and widespread international consensus. Moreover, violations of basic human rights can be precisely defined and are increasingly closely monitored. In many cases a determined effort by central political authorities could substantially reduce such violations. However, perhaps the worst abuses take place in countries torn by civil war, where government leaders have little control over the military and the police—not to mention armed irregulars and rampaging civilians.

With the important exception of countries in chaos, human rights abuses might be substantially reduced over time by a concerted international effort to deny aid to governments that were regular and substantial rights abusers. The recent European Community initiative moves toward establishing such a "global minimum standard," although it does not spell out precise conditions.

Although a coordinated donors' effort would have no direct leverage over wealthier governments, including those of some of the oil-rich countries, it might exercise indirect influence on such cases. And some of the governments that do rely substantially on aid might well alter their behavior. Unlike specific conditions, which quickly lose their effectiveness if they are not consistently and firmly enforced, a global standard can exercise a restraining influence on governments that think they might be targeted, even if they know that the principle is not entirely consistently enforced. International coordination would also put peer pressure on those donors most reluctant to sanction particular violators. And the possibility of coordinated international action would also provide an opening for the donor(s) closest to a particular government to take the lead in noting its concerns. The government, in turn, is likely to ask what it needs to do to avoid sanctions, translating the global standard into a discussion over specific actions. That dialogue may lead to suggestions for governmental actions and to aid for policy and institutional reforms. In such a scenario sanctions would not in fact be invoked but would nonetheless play a crucial role.

CONDITIONALITY FOR BROADENED PARTICIPATION AND COMPETITIVE DEMOCRACY

The goals of broadened participation and fuller political competition contrast with both human rights and economic governance in three key respects. First, the goal of respect for basic human rights (narrowly defined) seeks to restrain governments' behavior toward their citizens. Improved governance (narrowly interpreted) seeks certain standards of administrative behavior and accountability on the part of governments. Participation and competitive democracy, in contrast, require not only enabling action by governments but also motivation, organization, and appropriate behavior on the part of much of the society as a whole. How democratic reforms work out in practice will be largely shaped by the nature and degree of the organization of "civil society." For instance, decentralizing major aspects of government may have quite negative results if local society is controlled by exclusive and self-seeking elites. Similarly, if one or a few interest groups are powerful and well organized while others are not, sharply expanded scope for their political participation may severely bias public policy or paralyze the state.

Second, participation and democracy have much more inclusive, complex, and diffuse goals than human rights or improved economic governance. Participation, competitive politics, and representative governments can take a multitude of forms. The institutions and procedures that work well in one country may work very poorly in another. The risks of setting in motion seriously harmful dynamics are considerably greater with respect to participation and multiparty democracy than with respect to basic human rights and economic governance. And although new democracies can learn a great deal about institutional arrangements and procedures from more established systems, constructive patterns of participation and political competition require a great deal of hand-tailoring to fit specific cultural, social, and political traditions and circumstances.

Participation and increased political competition differ in a third way from the other major political goals on the international agenda. It is unlikely that the value and legitimacy of increased respect for human rights or improved governance are cast into question in countries where external pressure helped to bring reforms. But vigorous outside intervention to encourage participation and competitive democracy can jeopardize the legitimacy of those reforms.

These contrasts counsel a much more restrained use of conditionality to promote participation and democracy than to promote human rights or improved economic governance. There are a great many other ways outsiders can encourage responsible civic associations, press, judiciary, legislatures, parties, and fair elections. Most of the donors' recent policy statements stress dialogue, specially designed projects, and increased attention to the implications for participation and democracy of the full array of their activities.

However, specific or allocative conditionality might usefully support political liberalization in certain circumstances. Three seem particularly likely: 1) Breaking a specific policy bottleneck, keeping in mind the lessons from economic conditionality; 2) Punishing blatant antidemocratic moves to discourage similar actions elsewhere; and 3) More arguably, encouraging democratic breakthroughs by offering a temporary "democratic bonus."

Specific conditions designed to break a bottleneck blocking political liberalization might be appropriate if there is considerable pressure for reform within the country and the government, but action is blocked by a few powerful holdouts, and if the specific measures are within the control of central government officials and can be monitored. An example might be a change in laws or regulations on freedom of association. If donors force such action before there is substantial support, it is likely to be subverted in a variety of ways. It may also work to empower one or two particular interests or groups in ways that distort or undermine the participation of other groups. But where there is substantial support for such action, once taken it will rapidly become quite difficult to reverse. Moreover, changing regulations governing registration and the scope of action of civic associations is likely to be within the control of central political officials, and compliance with conditions can be easily monitored.

Serious backsliding or blatant antidemocratic steps—a military coup, an aborted or severely distorted election, perhaps a crackdown on civic associations or opposition parties—may also be appropriate situations for effective conditionality. One clear example was the U.S. intervention to protect the 1978 elections in the Dominican Republic. In that case early returns from the first fairly free elections in many years indicated that a candidate opposed by the military was likely to win. The vote count was suspended. Under pressure from President Carter, the count was resumed and the duly elected president took office. The desired action in this case had all the characteristics making it appropriate for conditionality: it could be taken by a few key people, was single-shot, and once taken, was self-sustaining. Moreover, there was a strong moral consensus both within the country and within the donor on the appropriateness of the action.

U.S. aid legislation has long provided for cutting off assistance in response to military coups. But the United States and other donors have not been at all consistent in this approach, nor have they normally coordinated their responses. The changing international setting increases the feasibility of coordinated donor action. A more consistent approach should be a more effective deterrent.

There are several well-recognized arguments against a preannounced, emphatic policy of cutting aid in such situations. All donors agree that the people of a country should not be punished for the behavior of their military or political leaders, and therefore that humanitarian aid channeled through nongovernmental organizations should be continued. It is also argued that cutting aid narrows opportunities for dialogue: however, other channels for dialogue remain available. A third argument is harder to resolve. Political liberalization is a long and difficult process, with many setbacks. If economic aid is raised or lowered in response to democratic ups and downs, an effective program of economic development becomes extremely difficult to administer. Moreover, if economic and social developments eventually prompt internal pressures for democratization (as, for instance, in Korea and Taiwan), then turning aid on and off interrupts the long-run processes underpinning democratization.

Therefore, the approach should be confined to one or two well-specified circumstances: military coups and perhaps aborted elections are obvious candidates. Some knowledgeable observers are uncomfortable even with such sharply focused negative conditionality. Some coups, they suggest, occur because civilian politics have reached a total impasse. The situation in Algeria in January 1992 offers a different scenario: an aborted election and virtual coup was staged to keep out of office a democratically elected government highly likely to subvert democratic processes and institutions. In short, some coups or aborted elections may be prodemocratic—or at least permit improved governance and economic growth, while sacrificing an empty shell of democratic process. The argument cannot be dismissed, and donors (individually and collectively) will not and should not substitute rigid criteria for judgment. But in much of the world, the possibility of coups adds to political instability and economic uncertainty. Reducing that possibility would promote both democratic consolidation and economic recovery. In short, there is a strong case for clear signals from the international community that coups are virtually never the best way to resolve difficulties.

Conditionality in the form of a "democracy bonus" may be a useful approach to promoting political liberalization in a third situation: where political forces are poised for or have just carried out a major democratic breakthrough. Donors' recent policy statements seem to imply such a bonus. It remains to be seen whether the donor community will be willing to offer significant aid increases on a consistent basis in response to democratic breakthroughs, especially to large and poor countries or to a number of countries simultaneously.

If they are in fact prepared to do so, further questions arise. Most aid projects, whether directly to support democratization or for broader economic support, take time to plan and set in motion. Nonproject aid for budget and import support can flow much more rapidly. But if the country needs extensive economic reform, a rapid rise in nonproject aid is likely to discourage prompt action. This is doubly unfortunate if the first few weeks or months of a new government offer the best political opening for painful economic reforms. Any democratic bonus therefore must be carefully designed and explicitly temporary, targeted to help the government during the difficult early period. One form a bonus might take is simply extra patience and flexibility from the donor community as the government balances economic and political pressures. If economic policies warrant, donors may provide a bonus in the form of significant debt relief, as was done in the case of Poland. Donors can also make clear that temporary programs to ease the social costs of adjustment will be prompt and generous. That course is easy if the country concerned is small and poor. It is much more costly if the country is large, and if the costs of adjustment bear heavily on a large working and middle class, as is true in most of Eastern Europe and the Soviet Union. But adequate aid to buffer social costs may be the most effective action outsiders can take to encourage successful consolidation of democratic openings.

In sum, conditionality may make a useful though limited contribution to both promoting respect for human rights and encouraging better economic governance, in combination with dialogue and project activities. Its role in promoting democracy is much more problematic, though it may be helpful in certain situations. For all three political objectives, but especially for promoting democracy, the appropriate mix of approaches varies with specific country circumstances, as the next section explores.

. . . .

CONDITIONALITY AS A TOOL IN VARYING COUNTRY CIRCUMSTANCES

■   MANY OF THE POINTS made earlier in this essay have implications for the kinds of country circumstances, as well as the particular reforms, for which conditionality may be appropriate and effective. Each country is of course unique, most are changing rapidly, and efforts to influence policy reforms must always be tailored to individual country circumstances. Nonetheless, there are certain basic points to take into account in considering the potential for conditional techniques.

AID DEPENDENCE

One key dimension is of course the degree of aid dependence. Countries with strong exports, as a result of oil or other natural resources or sustained good economic management, are not likely to be much influenced by conditions attached to aid. Trade sanctions may provide more leverage but raise a host of questions regarding the immediate self-interest of trading partners and the larger principles guiding international trade regimes. Sometimes, however, explicit governmental pressure may not be necessary. For example, Mexico recently released several high-profile political prisoners and established a human rights commission, in part in response to strong criticism from U.S. human rights groups. The leverage of private U.S. groups' criticism was heightened because Mexico feared that their pressures might jeopardize the much-desired Free Trade Agreement with the United States unless some reforms were evident.

ABILITY TO RESPOND TO EXTERNAL INFLUENCE

If some degree of aid dependence is a prerequisite for effective conditionality, so too is a recipient government capable of responding to external pressures. Countries torn by civil war, still raging or only recently and tentatively under control, usually cannot respond to such pressures because no government is clearly in power. As of early 1992, examples included Somalia, Sudan, Liberia, parts of Yugoslavia, and some members of the Commonwealth of Independent States. Angola, Mozambique, Ethiopia, Cambodia, and Lebanon were emerging from this situation.

In such circumstances, human rights abuses by governments and private groups are often particularly acute, while good governance and democratic procedures are distant abstractions. Aid should be and almost always is withheld, except for humanitarian programs. The rationale for withholding aid is not to exercise leverage on the government (which is not capable of responding), but because aid cannot be used effectively in such circumstances. Other nations, both industrial and developing, may look for opportunities for diplomatic intervention, and they may consider multi-lateral military intervention in extreme cases.

COMMITMENT TO REFORM

Among those countries that do rely to some extent on foreign aid, and have governments capable of responding to external influence, the probable effectiveness of conditionality is likely to reflect the degree of commitment to reform within the government, but not in a simple straight-line manner. Experience with encouraging economic reforms through conditioned aid suggests that real influence (though not necessarily immediate compliance) is likely to be greatest where reform-minded elements in the recipient government are neither very weak nor very strong. Where they are very weak, conditioned aid is not likely to produce real or sustained reforms, though if the aid is badly needed the government may go through the motions of compliance. At the other extreme, if reform elements within the government are very strong, conditions are largely superfluous.

In the most repressive authoritarian cases, most donors currently provide only limited humanitarian aid, or none at all. Examples include Haiti, Zaire, and Myanmar, as well as the communist "holdout" regimes in North Korea and Cuba. Withholding aid is not likely to prompt reform directly, but it at least avoids the appearance or actuality of propping up repressive regimes. In several of these cases prospects for effective use of aid for economic development are also very poor. However, a few highly authoritarian systems are serious and competent regarding economic development, for instance, Vietnam and China. These cases pose dilemmas for donors, especially for the multinational banks.

In a growing number of countries, long-established political elites remain in power and restrict political competition (with varying degrees of respect for human rights) but are moving toward increased participation and competition. Examples of such semi-authoritarian situations include a number of one- or no-party governments in Sub-Saharan Africa; some of the ex-communist nations in which reformist elements of the old communist elites remain in control, as in Albania, Romania, and several of the members of the Commonwealth of Independent States; and more arguably some long-established dominant-party systems in which opposition parties are legal but harassed and handicapped (as in Tunisia, Mexico, and Senegal).

Some of these semi-authoritarian governments, especially in Sub-Saharan Africa, are highly aid-dependent. In practice, specific political conditions are most likely to be directed to this group. Perhaps this is particularly appropriate, as many of these regimes have been kept in power over the past decades in large part because of external aid. But there can be no simple formula for effective conditions, even within this set of cases. They vary tremendously with respect to the strength of reformist pressures both within old elites and from popular forces. In some cases old elites are still widely viewed as legitimate or acceptable. As noted earlier, the nature and extent of organization in civil society will also affect the results of specific political reforms. Rapid political liberalization may release unsuspected capacities for organization and participation, as Eastern Europe has demonstrated. But liberalization may also release destructive conflicts, reinforce old inequalities, or entrench new biases in favor of particularly well-organized or vocal groups. Donors considering conditionality (as distinct from dialogue and support) cannot ignore these risks.

Most of the semi-authoritarian countries in the process of political liberalization also need considerable improvements in economic governance. Those goals can be pursued in conjunction with support for economic programs, and specific conditionality may well be useful.

Some of these nations pose particularly clear potential tensions between economic and political objectives. If Nigeria's rulers dilute economic reforms to keep the process of democratization on track, should aid be maintained? Conversely, how long should donors provide strong support for Ghana's vigorous economic reform efforts in the absence of parallel steps toward political liberalization?

The issue is not "simply" one of priorities. Also at issue are the interactions between political liberalization and economic adjustment. To what extent and in what ways do the two processes conflict in particular country circumstances? To what extent and in what ways are they complementary, even essential for each other? Responsible use of conditions to promote political reforms must rest on serious analysis of these questions.

The large and growing number of countries in which authoritarian governments have recently been replaced by elected governments offer a somewhat different set of circumstances. In contrast to the semi-authoritarian cases, in these "fragile reformers" new elites are in power and are committed in varying degrees to democratic consolidation. Most have little or no prior democratic history. A handful of these countries, mainly in Latin America but also including the Philippines and parts of Eastern Europe, have had some earlier experience with democracy. But the possibility of backsliding remains. In most, a wide range of reforms are needed to consolidate and sustain competitive and participatory politics and to improve governance. Although most of the new governments pose no systematic threats to human rights, ethnic and regional tensions among groups within the country may engender acute human rights abuses.

In most of these fragile reformers, donors are likely to rely primarily on dialogue and technical and financial support. In countries in which the military remains a political threat, a concerted and explicit donor policy of refusing to deal with governments put in place through coups might reduce the risks from that quarter. If donors are sufficiently committed, they might (singly or jointly) offer some form of temporary "democratic bonus" in the form of nonproject assistance, debt relief, or projects to relieve the social costs of economic adjustment. As discussed earlier, such a bonus would have to be designed to avoid conflict with pressure for necessary economic reforms, while perhaps making such reforms more palatable.

Some new democratic governments, or interim governments trying to move toward democracy, must cope with the aftermath of protracted civil wars, excessive military establishments, or numerous refugees. Generous assistance with the costs of demobilizing troops, rebuilding war-torn infrastructure, and resettling refugees is not precisely a "democracy bonus," yet such support clearly can be tremendously important in improving prospects for consolidation of democratic openings.

Fragile reformers may also occasionally offer opportunities for using conditionality to break specific bottlenecks. In these cases, however, there is an extra consideration that does not apply (or applies much less strongly) to similar opportunities in semi-authoritarian cases. In new democracies, outsiders' attempts to hasten reform may erode and weaken domestic forces, not because of the substance of the particular reforms being promoted, but because of the interference with internal democratic processes. Stated differently, in fragile new democracies it is particularly important that the government and the people of the country control the choice of measures and tactics for the consolidation of democracy. They must own the process as well as the objective.

This last consideration applies also in a somewhat different set of circumstances, that is, in countries with established democratic systems, where governmental commitment to democracy is not in question and the basic institutions and procedures are well established. Some nations that fit this description nonetheless face acute strains from the demands of economic adjustment, drug and terrorist gangs, or ethnic extremists. Examples include Colombia, Sri Lanka, and Venezuela. In these circumstances, with respect to political issues, outsiders should rely almost wholly on dialogue and support. Political conditionality is inappropriate, not only because it is little needed, but because it would interfere with the country's own reasonably strong democratic processes. (As in all categories, where governance needs improving, specific conditions may well be appropriate).

REGIONAL CONTRASTS

Each geographic region is politically diverse. But the distribution or mix of firmly authoritarian governments, semi-authoritarian systems in the process of reform, fragile new democracies, and established democracies varies greatly across regions. The scope and nature of conditionality, and more broadly the approaches likely to effectively promote political reform, therefore also vary considerably by region.

In Latin America, in early 1992, only three countries (Cuba, Haiti, and Guyana) are ruled by governments that were not put in place by reasonably fair elections. (Elections are scheduled later in 1992 for Guyana.) In Mexico, however, the 1988 election was questioned, and opposition parties and groups continue to be harassed. More generally, elected governments are precarious in many countries, most clearly in Central America. Many governments are struggling with an acute "crisis of the state," compounded by prolonged and severe fiscal problems and administrative decay. Most of the established democracies as well as the fragile reformers face serious strains from economic adjustment and, in several cases, from drug and terrorist groups. The challenge is one of consolidation and reform in accord with changing demands and concepts of the state. The role of conditionality (other than that aimed at promoting improved governance) is quite limited.

Much of the Middle East remains authoritarian, and prospects for reform are slight in the near future. Asia offers a more mixed profile and raises rather different issues. Two large and important authoritarian nations—China and Indonesia—have been strong economic performers and have also pursued quite effective pro-poor strategies. Three semi-authoritarian nations—Korea, Singapore, and less clearly Thailand—also have good growth and equity records; all are making sporadic progress toward political liberalization. Both growth and political stability in the established democracies of India and Sri Lanka have been less impressive, while Bangladesh and Pakistan have vacillated between weak democratic governments and military regimes. With these points in mind, it is quite understandable that many Asian commentators argue for a phased-in approach—pursuing economic growth before introducing political democracy, along the lines demonstrated by Taiwan and Korea. At the World Bank and USAID, views in the Asia regional offices are considerably more cautious about pressure for political reforms (and particularly for political competition) than are those held by their counterparts working on Latin America and Africa.

Country circumstances in Africa range from civil war or recalcitrant authoritarian systems to a few established democracies (including Botswana and Mauritius), but most countries are in the process of haltingly introducing some political liberalization or have recently put new reformist governments in office. Almost everywhere the tasks of broadening and deepening civic society and developing an understanding of the roles and limits of responsible political competition are immense, as are the challenges of improved economic governance. Because so many African nations are small and almost all are poor, they are also more uniformly aid-dependent and more subject to donor leverage. The region probably offers the greatest temptation for donors to seek to accelerate political as well as economic reforms through attempted conditionality. Yet it may also be the region in which analytic and administrative capabilities are the thinnest, and networks of grassroots and intermediate associations the least developed. Extensive use of conditionality in such circumstances externalizes responsibility and may undermine the longer-run processes of learning and organization crucial to support improved governance, participation, and responsible political competition. In short, political conditionality may be easiest for donors in Africa, but should be used with special care.

BEYOND THE CONDITIONALITY MODE

■   AS NOTED EARLIER, conditionality is always resented as an invasion of sovereignty, an explicit or implicit claim that the donor knows best, and a tacit reflection of power inequalities. From the perspective of the donor or lender as well, conditional aid is complex and costly to administer. Conditionality creates tensions with recipients, and often within the donor agency and government as well. Conditionality also limits flexibility, in the sense of the ability to respond rapidly and easily to changed circumstances.

But conditionality is not likely to diminish much in the 1990s. Indeed, in view of donors' multiple new goals and growing pressure from groups with political leverage on the aid agencies, conditionality may well increase. Precisely because of that fact, it is worth thinking about the possibilities for moving beyond modes of dialogue and conditionality where a single recipient interacts with a single donor, or with multiple donors coordinating their aid (as in consultative groups). Truly multilateral approaches that involve recipients in determining the criteria for aid may generate more genuine commitment in recipient countries, more constructive exchange of experience among them, and less abrasive relations between donor and recipient nations. A further logical extension of that approach is to engage recipients in monitoring each other's performance according to agreed criteria and principles.

History offers some partial precedents for such approaches. The Marshall Plan engaged the war-torn nations of post-World War II Europe in reciprocal assessment of needs and monitoring of policies and progress as criteria for allocation of U.S. assistance. The Alliance for Progress entailed a mutually selected Committee of Nine responsible with their staff for monitoring and criticizing progress toward broad social and economic goals in each country in Latin America. In the initial years of the alliance, allocation of U.S. assistance was partly guided by these assessments.

For such an approach to work, the aid-receiving nations probably must share the perception that their future prospects are partly interdependent. A sense of linked destinies provides both motivation for taking an interest in other nations' internal policies and performance, and a rationale for accepting some degree of monitoring and criticism regarding one's own affairs from governments not in a position to offer financial support. (Note that a sense of interdependence need not imply warm relations: often, indeed, interdependence generates tensions.) Moreover, a fully multilateral approach is probably easier if the donors involved also see the set of recipients as interdependent.

Consistent with that hypothesis, Central America currently provides perhaps the clearest evidence of tentative movement toward a genuinely multilateral approach, involving coordination in setting of targets among recipients as well as donors. Moreover, the consultation encompasses not only economic policies and programs but also (in a modest degree) political reforms.

The San José accords have been the main channel for such consultation. The accords were initiated in 1984 as a forum for discussion between Central American governments and the European Community and its member governments. Initially focused on security and peacemaking, the annual ministerial-level meetings more recently have emphasized issues of development, regional integration, and democratization. The Central American foreign ministers meet in advance of the annual conference to coordinate their positions.

By the late 1980s their consultation was reinforced by the evolving "Esquipulas process," which entailed the five Central American presidents coming together at six- or eight-month intervals to discuss issues of common concern. Initiated by President Oscar Arias of Costa Rica as a channel for promoting regional peace, the meetings have shifted increasingly to problems of recovery and growth. The presidential meetings provide an opportunity for review at the highest level of the positions agreed upon by the five foreign ministers in preparation for the annual meetings with European donors.

In 1991 the United States proposed a new forum for bringing together the Central Americans, and the governments and international agencies providing aid to the region. The Partnership for Democracy and Development in Central America (PDD) includes not only the 12 European Community nations that take part in the San José accords, but also the additional members of the Organization for Economic Cooperation and

Development (OECD), the United States, Canada, and Japan, plus Colombia, Mexico, and Venezuela as "friends of Central America," and various international organizations. On the recipient side, Panama and Belize are represented in addition to the five Central American nations. The PDD initiative prompted skepticism among both Central Americans and Europeans. Not only does it overlap with the San José arrangement, but many suspected that it is a smoke screen for rapidly dwindling U.S. assistance to the region. Nonetheless, the PDD is certainly more broadly inclusive than the San José process.

Two major meetings have now taken place within the PDD framework. For this study, it is particularly interesting that the PDD operates through two committees (each with donor and recipient participation), focused respectively on economic development and democracy. The committee on democracy has identified several areas appropriate for external support, including strengthening the administration of justice, human rights, and legislative and electoral institutions, as well as reintegration of persons displaced by regional strife. The PDD, like the San José accords, seems to be reinforcing and accelerating autonomous regional trends toward increased coordination. Without exaggerating their contribution, both multilateral arrangements are encouraging the Central Americans themselves to identify specific problems and targets for reform, to set goals, and to monitor each other's progress to some degree. The degree to which these multilateral arrangements will eventually become a major channel for assistance, either replacing or substantially reshaping bilateral aid relationships, remains an open question.

No other regional or subregional grouping currently seems to provide so clear an example of multilateral donor and recipient collaboration, including an explicit focus on political reforms. Human rights, good governance, and democracy are part of the agenda for discussion in a great many multilateral forums, including the United Nations and its various agencies and commissions, the English-speaking Commonwealth, Francophonie, the Organization of American States, and the Organization of African Unity. All of these are much too large and diffuse to play as concrete a role as the emerging Central American arrangements. Nor are these organizations normally involved in determining criteria for programming aid or trade arrangements, though the OAS has taken responsibility for coordinating members' responses to the situation in Haiti.

While also very large, the Lomé Convention moves beyond discussion to mutually agreed and reciprocal responsibilities. Lomé IV, signed in December 1989, spells out a framework for cooperation on a range of aid, trade, and related issues between the members of the European Community and 70 nations of Sub-Saharan Africa, the Caribbean, and the Pacific. More than a year of discussions and negotiations preceded Lomé IV, providing a forum for dialogue not only on specific technical questions, but also on broader concerns such as the implications of closer European integration and of events in Eastern Europe. Among these issues were human rights and increased popular participation in development. Addressing the convention in December 1989, Michel Rocard, then president of the Council of the European Community, noted explicitly that "[T]he requirements of democracy and social justice to which the twelve Member States have pledged themselves are no different from those we plan to observe in our relations with the ACP [Africa, Caribbean and Pacific] states."[47]

Each developing nation participating in the convention draws up a "national indicative program" as a basis for programming the aid provided by the European Community (EC) within the Lomé framework. The programming process provides a further, country-specific channel for dialogue regarding reciprocal obligations and may reflect the growing EC emphasis on political reforms in some instances. This process is essentially bilateral (between each recipient and the European Community as a multinational donor). However, individual countries' positions are probably somewhat influenced by the themes stressed in the earlier multilateral discussions and will also feed into those discussions at the next iteration. In the long run, the framework and the process may well increase consensus between the EC and many of the recipients and enhance "ownership" of reforms by the recipients, as compared to simple bilateral relationships in the absence of the multilateral framework.

The recently established Global Coalition for Africa is intended as still another arena for more open and egalitarian dialogue between wealthy and poor nations on a range of development issues. The coalition was established in 1991 with support from bilateral donors (especially the Dutch and Norwegians) and the World Bank. It has the advantage of being somewhat smaller and less unwieldy than the forums already mentioned, but the considerable handicap of having very little aid to dispense. The coalition's steering committee includes 30 ministerial-level members, 10 each from donor nations, African governments, and regional and global international financial institutions. The coalition is intended as a forum for resolving political and major policy issues that emerge from the array of North-South technical agencies working in Africa. There are also plans to work, through the United Nations Development Programme, with governments and private groups in individual African nations to formulate long-term "perspective studies" as a basis for expanded and more consensual dialogues between donors and recipients.

Even if old and new multilateral arenas do not move beyond the discussion stage to take some role in allocating aid and monitoring performance, they are likely to serve an additional purpose: highlighting some of the actions the industrial democracies should take within their own boundaries to promote the goals of the new international agenda.

Poorer nations are well aware that most industrial democracies could pursue considerably more aggressive policies for environmental protection and arms expenditure reductions at home, to their own benefit and that of developing countries. Beyond that general point, poorer nations note that some of the industrialized nations' policies and practices inadvertently or even deliberately discourage reforms in poorer nations. Progress toward reduced corruption, for example, is hampered by the propensity of industrial nations' investors and traders to play along with corrupt officials in developing nations: industrial democracies could adopt and enforce stricter regulations on such practices. Some donor nation agencies and programs work at odds with others: U.S. drug enforcement or military missions, for instance, often quietly but explicitly signal to their developing-country counterparts that they will wink at human rights abuses. Increased multilateral discussion of political reforms in poorer countries is likely to increase pressure on the wealthy nations for greater consistency in their own actions.

CONCLUSIONS

■   THROUGHOUT HISTORY, oppressive government has been one major cause for human suffering. In the 1990s, long-run trends and international events have converged to generate widespread pressures for political reforms. The possibilities seem brighter now than in many decades for significant improvements in governments' respect for human rights, responsible governance, and participatory democracy. Encouraging such improvements should be among the top foreign policy objectives of the United States and other industrial democracies. How best to do so is a question now drawing a great deal of attention. This essay focuses on one aspect of that larger question: the use of conditions attached to aid.

Conditionality can make significant contributions to encouraging improved governance, respect for human rights, and more extensive democratic participation and competition. Used well, conditionality is a useful adjunct to dialogue and persuasion, and to direct and indirect support for political reforms. Conditions attached to aid can reinforce reformers within recipient countries, focus the attention and maintain the resolve of governments, accelerate some decisions and shape their design. Conditionality can sometimes promote debate and revised assumptions within a country even when the government does not comply with the particular conditions. Measurement and monitoring go along with conditionality, and fuller and more precise information is helpful to reformers within and outside of aid-receiving countries, even if there is no immediate improvement in performance.

Conditionality is a supplement to other approaches, however, not a strategy. It is a much more constrained instrument than dialogue and support. Unlike these other instruments, conditionality has little impact in countries that are not dependent on aid. Its use is also more likely than that of other methods to conflict with donors' other foreign policy objectives. The real influence of conditionality on governments' behavior is problematic. Specific conditions may be met while their intent is evaded. Where compliance is strong, the reason often is that the government was already strongly committed to reform; the conditions may have been largely redundant.

Moreover, conditionality carries costs. It may deflect the dialogue between donor and recipient from substance to procedure and bargaining. It may undermine officials' sense of responsibility for their own actions and their country's progress. Conditionality can also discredit desirable reforms by making them appear externally imposed. Moreover, designing, monitoring, and enforcing conditions can consume a great deal of donor time and resources that might perhaps be better put toward other tasks, including developing a deepened grasp of interactions between economic and political reforms, broader contacts within the recipient country, and more imaginative design of projects to support improved governance and democratic reform.

In short, some of the apparent attractions of conditionality to donor governments (and their publics and concerned NGOs) are illusory. Conditionality sometimes gives the appearance of decisive action appropriate to the importance of the goals, but it is often less powerful than it appears. Conditionality certainly is not a way to circumvent the long and difficult but essential process of building consensus and commitment within recipient nations. And although conditionality appears to be an inexpensive way to exert influence, it can carry significant hidden costs. The challenge, then, is to use the instrument for appropriate objectives, in circumstances in which its potential benefits exceed its costs, and in productive combination with other approaches.

Donors' new policies emphasize allocative rather than specific conditionality. They seek to encourage political reform by shifting the distribution of aid to favor reforming governments. The approach is attractive because it is less confrontational and interventionist than more specific conditions such as those used by the IMF or the World Bank to promote economic reforms. But donors are not likely to pursue a consistent general strategy of allocating aid to reflect political reforms. A less consistent, more ad hoc pattern will emerge, in which significant changes in political performance lead to penalties or bonuses in countries that are not of primary importance to the donors' other foreign policy objectives. Penalties are likely to be somewhat clearer and more consistent than bonuses, because most donors' budgets are tight and because sizable nonproject bonuses (as distinct from various projects to help support and consolidate political liberalization) may interfere with economic conditionality. The donor community can and should send fairly clear signals that major abuses of human rights, military coups, and aborted elections are almost always unacceptable. With respect to most other actions, however, the development of clear-cut global standards is much less probable. In practice, allocative or global conditionality is likely to translate into specific conditionality.

How can this "realistic prospect" of the forms conditionality will take be focused to maximize conditionality's contribution to political reform? Four sets of recommendations emerge.

1) *Conditionality is best suited to emphasize improved economic governance and human rights; it should be used with greater caution with respect to competitive democracy.*

■ Some aspects of improved governance are particularly closely linked to ongoing goals of economic recovery, growth, and increased equity. External pressure for such reforms is often more readily accepted because of the links to accepted donor concerns. The specific targets vary among countries. Some may be appropriate for specific conditionality, keeping in mind the lessons from experience discussed earlier and reviewed below.

■ Respect for fundamental human rights offers the best prospects for internationally coordinated action by donors, who should reduce or withdraw aid from the most serious offenders.

■ Conditionality may help to discourage backsliding with respect to competitive democracy. Specifically, donors should adopt a coordinated strategy of penalizing virtually all military coups and most instances of aborted elections, although there may occasionally be valid reasons for the latter. Other than to discourage backsliding, dialogue and support are generally more appropriate techniques than conditionality for promoting broadened participation and competitive politics.

2) *Design specific conditions with the lessons of experience in mind.*

■ Is the desired reform within the control of a small number of host-government officials?

- Is the measure clearly specified, and can it be objectively monitored?

- What additional actions (inside or outside the government) are essential if the reform is to have its desired effect, and are those actions likely to be taken?

- From the donor's perspective, is the reform of sufficiently high priority to warrant the costs of withholding aid if the condition is not met? Is there clear agreement within the donor government or international agency on this point?

3) *Reserve conditionality for appropriate country circumstances.*

- A country that cannot control its own territory or is preoccupied with civil war is hardly in a position to implement political conditions—or to use almost any development assistance effectively.

- Where old authoritarian elites are still in power, the value of conditionality depends on the strength of reform elements within the elite. Conditions are probably most useful in prompting reforms when the reformers are neither very weak nor just about to take over power, and when the reforms are likely to generate their own self-sustaining reactions within the society.

- In new (and usually fragile) democracies and in established democracies, dialogue and support are usually more helpful than specific conditions, although some economic governance measures may be appropriate targets of conditionality. In both new and established democracies, use of conditions to prompt political reforms may taint the legitimacy of the reforms themselves.

- In fragile new democracies, an explicitly temporary "democracy bonus" may be useful. The bonus should be designed to ease transition costs without weakening incentives for necessary economic reforms. In new democracies that inherited large military establishments or have recently emerged from civil wars, or where there are large numbers of refugees, generous assistance with the costs of demobilizing troops or resettling refugees may also improve prospects for consolidating democracy.

4) *Donors should coordinate closely with each other regarding political objectives, most urgently with respect to penalties for serious human rights abuses, military coups, and aborted elections.*

■ In the post-Cold War setting, a high degree of donor coordination is almost surely feasible with respect to major human rights abuses, and will often be feasible in response to military coups and aborted elections. The DAC and the European Community are already moving vigorously in that direction. The impetus should be sustained.

■ Coordination among donors with respect to bonuses or increased support for major political reforms is desirable, but less urgent and probably a good deal more difficult.

■ Coordinated action with respect to other specific reforms will often be difficult and is not essential. The World Bank is likely to take the lead in encouraging specific steps toward improved economic governance in many cases. Donors should let each other know about their priorities, targets, and the rationale for these, to avoid inadvertent conflicts and encourage coordinated dialogue and support. Occasionally coordinated specific conditionality may make sense. Consultative groups provide an obvious forum for such consultation.

Wealthy democracies seeking to encourage political reforms should also be seeking to move beyond the standard conditionality mode to involve recipient governments and private groups in defining and monitoring political reform targets. Political reforms will emerge and become sustainable as governments and private groups become convinced that they are desirable and deepen their understanding of the discipline and trade-offs required. Evolving international norms and growing knowledge of others' experiences can help the process along. For some sets of countries or subregions, multilateral forums in which recipients are encouraged to develop "collective ownership" of political reforms might be an important supplement to more general debate in larger forums, and a partial substitute for conditionality imposed by donors singly or collectively.

If donors seek to influence and encourage political reforms in poorer nations, they need also to look more closely at their own practices and policies, especially those that bear directly on developing nations and interfere with desired reforms. More genuinely multilateral approaches are likely to focus attention on such issues as conflicting signals from different segments of donors' foreign policy establishments, and the role of foreign business in perpetuating corrupt practices in developing nations.

Serious attention to such inconsistencies would directly support political reforms in poorer nations. More consistent actions by the governments of wealthy nations would also increase the credibility and acceptability of their efforts to encourage much more difficult and painful reforms in poorer nations.

Notes

[1] This view was most clearly and forcefully stated in the World Bank's long-term perspective study, *Sub-Saharan Africa: From Crisis to Sustainable Growth* (Washington, DC: 1990).

[2] For reviews of the evidence, see Atul Kohli, "Democracy and Development," in *Development Strategies Reconsidered*, U.S.-Third World Policy Perspectives No. 5 (New Brunswick, NJ: Transaction Publishers in cooperation with the Overseas Development Council, 1986), pp. 154-162; Joan M. Nelson, "Political Participation," in Myron Weiner and Samuel P. Huntington, *Understanding Political Development* (Boston: Little Brown, 1987), pp. 141-144; John Healy, "The Contribution of Political Reform to Economic Progress," paper prepared for a conference on governance in Africa, Wilton Park, Great Britain, January 1992.

[3] Asian experience includes a number of cases of dramatic economic growth under authoritarian regimes, and the view that such regimes may be particularly well suited to promote development, at least in its earlier stages, persists among many Asians and Asian scholars.

[4] Mark Robinson, "Aid and Political Reform" (London: Overseas Development Institute, January 1992), ODI Briefing Paper, p. 4.

[5] *Marches Tropicaux*, January 12, 1990, p. 87; *Le Monde*, March 3, 1990; *Marches Tropicaux*, June 29, 1991, pp. 1833-35. On Benin, see Michael Bratton and Nicolas van der Walle, "Popular Protest and Political Reform in Africa," in *Governance and Politics in Africa*, Goran Hyden and Michael Bratton, eds. (Boulder, CO: Lynne Rienner Press, 1991).

[6] *Financial Times*, October 1, 1990, p. 4.

[7] Klemens van de Sand and Ralf M. Mohs, "Neue politische Kriterien des BMZ," *E + Z* (October 1991), pp. 4-5.

[8] *Informatie* (information bulletin published by the Dutch Ministry of Cooperation), No. 17/e, September 1990.

[9] *Japan Digest*, April 22, 1991, p. 11; *FBIS-EAS* 91-071, April 12, 1991, p. 7.

[10] World Bank, *Managing Development: The Governance Dimension* (Washington, DC: World Bank, 1991), p.v.

[11] Development Assistance Committee 30th High-Level Meeting, "Resolution of the Council and of the Member States Meeting in the Council on Human Rights, Democracy, and Development," various pages.

[12] The U.S. Department of State and other western governments condemned the killings and called for a thorough investigation. The Indonesian government conducted an inquiry and

announced the firing of two military commanders in the region. The Netherlands and Canada suspended aid, prompting Indonesia to declare it would not accept aid entailing human rights conditions. See Gordon Hein, "U.S.-Indonesia Relations Enter a More Complex Era" (San Francisco: Center for Asian Pacific Affairs of the Asia Foundation, February 1992), CAPA Report No. 6, p. 2; and the *Nikkei* (Japan Economic Journal), February 16, 1992.

[13] Christopher Madison, "The New Democratizers," *National Journal* (December 7, 1991), p. 2967.

[14] Speech by Lynda Chalker to the Overseas Development Institute at Chatham House, London, June 25, 1991.

[15] John W. Sewell and Peter M. Storm, *United States Budget for a New World Order: Promoting National Security and Advancing America's Interests Abroad FY1992* (Washington, DC: Overseas Development Council, 1991).

[16] Jane Perlez, "Ethiopia Unable to Get U.S. Aid Despite Reforms," *The New York Times*, March 2, 1992.

[17] In January 1992, Germany claimed to be providing 70 percent of all Western aid to the newly independent republics of the former Soviet Union, although much of that aid was used to pay for the removal, retraining, and relocation of Soviet troops stationed in East Germany. Marc Fisher, "Bonn on Russian Aid: Put Up or Shut Up," *The Washington Post*, January 16, 1992.

[18] Abraham F. Lowenthal, *Exporting Democracy: The United States and Latin America: Part One* (Baltimore: The Johns Hopkins Press, 1991), p. 95; Samuel P. Huntington, *The Third Wave: Democratization in the Late Twentieth Century* (Norman, OK, and London: University of Oklahoma Press, 1991), p. 98.

[19] Center for International Policy, "Military Aid Law," *International Policy Report*, Washington, DC, 1991.

[20] Center for International Policy, "Economic Aid Law," *International Policy Report*, Washington, DC, 1991.

[21] For a review of the general legislation, see David Forsythe, "The Fate of General Legislation," *Human Rights Quarterly*, Vol. 9, 1987.

[22] Ibid., pp. 400-402.

[23] Michael Stohl, David Carleton, and Steven E. Johnson, "Human Rights and U.S. Foreign Assistance from Nixon to Carter," *Journal of Peace Studies*, Vol. 21, No. 3, 1984.

[24] Jeane Kirkpatrick, "Dictatorships and Double Standards," *Commentary*, Vol. 68, No. 5, 1979.

[25] See Tamar Jacoby, "Reagan's Turnaround on Human Rights," *Foreign Affairs*, Vol. 64, No. 5, Summer 1986; David P. Forsythe, "Human Rights in U.S. Foreign Policy: Retrospect and Prospect," *Political Science Quarterly*, Vol. 105, No. 3, 1990, p. 442; and A. Glenn Mower Jr., *Human Rights and American Foreign Policy: The Carter and Reagan Experiences* (Westport, CT: Greenwood Press, Inc., 1987), p. 50.

[26] For a discussion of country-specific legislation, see David Forsythe, "Congress and Human Rights Legislation: An Overview," in *Human Rights and US Foreign Policy: Congress Reconsidered* (Gainsville, FL: University of Florida Press, 1988), and Lawyers Committee for Human Rights, "Linking Security Assistance and Human Rights" (New York: 1989), pp. 28-40.

[27] David Forsythe, *Human Rights and U.S. Foreign Policy: Congress Reconsidered*, op. cit., p. 16.

[28] Center for International Policy, "Military Aid Law," op. cit., p. 6, and Lawyers Committee for Human Rights, "Linking Security Assistance and Human Rights," pp. 31-34.

[29] Center for International Policy, "Multilateral Aid Law" *International Policy Report*, Washington, DC, 1991, pp. 5-8.

[30] See *The New York Times* article on the Human Rights Watch 1991 Report, December 30, 1991.

[31] Patrick J. Flood, "U.S. Human Rights Initiatives Concerning Argentina" in *The Diplomacy of Human Rights*, David D. Newsom, ed. (Lanham, MD: University Press of America, 1986).

[32] Many researchers during the last decade have sought to test empirically whether human rights concerns influence U.S. foreign aid decisions. Despite the stated human rights policy, most of the quantitative studies found no clear relationship between the allocation of U.S. assistance and the human rights records of aid recipients. One early study revealed a positive relationship—the more U.S. aid provided, the more repressive the recipient government. Another study, using a more sophisticated model, examined the "gatekeeping" stage, when policymakers decide which countries will receive foreign aid, as well as the levels of assistance. The study, though later widely critiqued, concluded that human rights concerns do influence aid allocations in certain cases. The research illustrates various methodological weaknesses inherent in empirical analysis of human rights policy, including the quantitative measurement of human rights. The question of how long it takes for human rights atrocities in a recipient country to be reflected in the U.S. foreign aid appropriations is also troublesome. For more information, see the following studies: Lars Schoultz, "U.S. Foreign Policy and Human Rights Violations in Latin America," *Comparative Politics*, Vol. 13, January 1981; Stohl, Carleton, and Johnson, "Human Rights and U.S. Foreign Assistance from Nixon to Carter," op. cit.; David L. Cingranelli and Thomas E. Pasquarello, "Human Rights Practices and the Distribution of U.S. Foreign Aid to Latin American Countries," *American Journal of Political Science*, Vol. 29, August, 1985; David Carleton and Michael Stohl, "The Role of Human Rights in U.S. Foreign Assistance Policy: A Critique and Reappraisal," *American Journal of Political Science*, Vol. 31 November 1987; James M. McCormick and Neil Mitchell, "Is U.S. Aid Really Linked to Human Rights and Foreign Assistance, An Update," *Social Science Quarterly*, Vol. 70, No. 4, December 1989; Steven C. Poe, "Human Rights and U.S. Foreign Aid: A Review of Quantitative Studies and Suggestions for Future Research," *Human Rights Quarterly*, Vol. 12, 1990; Daniel Hofrenning, "Human Rights and Foreign Aid: A Comparison of the Reagan and Carter Administrations," *American Politics Quarterly*, Vol. 18, No. 4, October 1990; Steven C. Poe, "Human Rights and the Allocation of U.S. Military Assistance," *Journal of Peace Research*, Vol. 28, No. 2, May 1991.

[33] *Amnesty International Report 1991* (London: Amnesty International Publications, 1991), p. 290.

[34] "Military Aid Law," op. cit., p. 15; and "Human Rights Watch World Report 1990: Americas Section," New York, January 1991, p.9.

[35] Katarina Tomasevski, *Development Aid and Human Rights* (New York: St. Martin's Press, 1989), pp. 49-57.

[36] World Bank, *Annual Report 1990* (Washington, DC: World Bank), p.54.

[37] Correspondence to the author from Robert W. Russell, Chief, External Relations Department, May 17, 1991.

[38] World Bank, *Report on Adjustment Lending II: Policies for the Recovery of Growth* (Washington, DC: World Bank, March 1990), Table 4.3, p.44.

[39] For a fuller discussion, see Paul Mosley, Jane Harrigan, and John Toye, *Aid and Power: The World Bank and Policy-Based Lending* (London and New York: Routledge, 1991), pp. 135-137, 166-167.

[40] Eliot Berg Associates, *Adjustment Postponed: Economic Policy Reform in Senegal in the 1980s*, report prepared for USAID/DAKAR (Alexandria, VA: Eliot Berg Associates, October 1990), p. 220.

[41] World Bank, *Adjustment Lending: An Evaluation of Ten Years of Experience* (Washington, DC: World Bank, 1988), p. 89.

[42] Eliot Berg Associates, op. cit.

[43] For a discussion of these points in Africa, see David Gordon, "Conditionality in Policy-Based Donor Assistance in Africa: Assessing and Learning from Recent Experience," forthcoming in Paul Mosley, ed., *Development Finance and Policy Reform* (London: MacMillan, 1992).

[44] For examples, Lynda Chalker speech, op. cit.; and Klemens van de Sand and Ralf M. Mohs, op. cit.

[45] See Thomas J. Biersteker, "The New Conditionality: Linking External Assistance to Political Reforms in Developing Countries" University of Southern California, unpublished manuscript, April 1991, for a typology distinguishing various phases of economic and political reform and their interactions. For an excellent more general discussion of interactions between economic reform and consolidation of democratic transitions, see Adam Przeworski, *Democracy and the Market: Political and Economic Reforms in Eastern Europe and Latin America* (Cambridge, NY: Cambridge University Press, 1991), especially Chapter 4.

[46] The idea of "Integrity International" is suggested in Pierre Landell-Mills and Ismail Serageldin, "Governance and the External Factors," World Bank Annual Conference on Development Economics 1991, Washington, DC, April 25–26, 1991.

[47] "Lomé IV Convention," *The Courier*, No. 120, March-April 1990, p. 6.

Acknowledgements

The authors would like to thank the many people who contributed to the development of this study through extensive interviews and comments on earlier versions, including Nicole Ball, Robert Charlick, Ford Cooper, Richard Feinberg, Muni Figueres, Paul George, Bryan Hehir, Barrie Ireton, Geoffrey Lamb, Carol Lancaster, Sarwar Lateef, Michael Morfit, Peter Mountfield, Stacy Rhodes, Tina Rosenberg, Sylvia Saborio, John Sewell, William Schoux, Roy Stacey, Peter Storm, and Ann Williams.

About the Authors

JOAN M. NELSON is a Senior Associate of the Overseas Development Council. Her work at ODC during the past several years has focused on the politics of economic stabilization and adjustment, and most recently on links between market-oriented economic reforms and democratization in Second and Third World nations. She worked with the policy planning division of USAID during the mid-1960s. Later she taught at Massachusetts Institute of Technology and co-directed a research program on political participation in developing nations at the Harvard Center for International Affairs. From 1974 to 1982 she established and directed the program in Comparative Politics and Modernization at the Johns Hopkins School of Advanced International Studies. She has consulted for the World Bank, USAID, and the International Monetary Fund on problems of governance and the politics of economic adjustment, and on rural-to-urban migration. During the mid-1980s she served as a member of the National Academy of Science Population Committee. Among her publications are *Aid, Influence, and Foreign Policy* (MacMillan 1968); *No Easy Choice: Political Participation in Developing Countries* (Harvard 1976); *Access to Power: Politics and the Urban Poor* (Princeton 1979); *Fragile Coalitions: The Politics of Economic Adjustment* (Overseas Development Council 1989); and *Economic Crisis and Policy Choice* (Princeton 1990).

STEPHANIE J. EGLINTON is a Project Assistant at the Overseas Development Council. She holds a degree in International Relations from Tufts University. She has worked for the U.S. House of Representatives and has traveled and studied in Central America.

About the ODC

The Overseas Development Council's programs focus on U.S. relations with developing countries in five broad policy areas: U.S. foreign policy and developing countries in a post-Cold War era; international finance and easing the debt crisis; international trade during the Uruguay Round, and beyond; development strategies and development cooperation; and environment and development.

Within these major policy themes, ODC seeks to increase American understanding of the economic and social problems confronting the developing countries and to promote awareness of the importance of these countries to the United States in an increasingly interdependent international system. In pursuit of these goals, ODC functions as:

■ A center for policy analysis. Bridging the worlds of ideas and actions, ODC translates the best academic research and analysis on selected issues of policy importance into information and recommendations for policymakers in the public and private sectors.

■ A forum for the exchange of ideas. ODC's conferences, seminars, workshops, and briefings brings together legislators, business executives, scholars, and representatives of international financial institutions and non-governmental groups.

■ A resource for public education. Through its publications, meetings, testimony, lectures, and formal and informal networking, ODC makes timely, objective, non-partisan information available to an audience that includes but reaches far beyond the Washington policymaking community.

Board of Directors

CHAIR

STEPHE
The Equ
Societ

ES
Exchange
R
stitution

E
ollege

VICE C

WAYNE
Institute
Educa

RUTH
Larchm

AS

Inc.
N

CHAIF

THEOD
Univers

ROBER
Washin

VICTO
The Pa

opment

RP
mbly

PRES

JOHN
Overse

Inc.
AYLOR
d
c.

DIRE

MICF
Arent

MAR
Bern

GOL
How
of

ANT
Endi

TERS
sity

ILSON, III
earch on
velopment
lichigan

WIRTHLIN
iroup

ons provided
ification only.